I0616921

I Love You, I Hate You!

HEALING GENERATIONAL BONDS: NAVIGATING THE MOTHER-DAUGHTER RELATIONSHIP.

From Rampant Feline Media

I LOVE YOU! I HATE YOU!

HEALING GENERATIONAL BONDS:
NAVIGATING THE MOTHER-DAUGHTER
RELATIONSHIP.

Publisher: Rampant Feline Media/Betsy Chasse
www.betsychasse.net

Authored by: Beatrice Andrade, Betsy Chasse, Patricia L. Lai, Claudia Micco, Alli Nathan, Catherine Stilo, Dr. Theresa L. Smith, D.C., Tara Fries, Karen Emi Fujii, Christine Judal, Caroline A. Janssens, Shelley Whizin, Sarah Schultz, Heidi Zin

© 2024 All Rights Reserved

ISBN Paperback: 979-8-9910714-6-8
ISBN EBook: 979-8-9910714-7-5

Table of Contents

Foreword By Judy Wilkins-Smith *6*

Introduction By Betsy Chasse *11*

Chapter 1
Hell On Heels: Nice Women Do Not Divorce By Claudia Micco *14*

Chapter 2
The Eyes Of An Old Mother By Catherine Stilo *20*

Chapter 3
Oh, The Tangled Webs We Weave! By Dr. Theresa L. Smith, D.C. *28*

Chapter 4
Echoes of an Undreamt Life By Karen Emi Fujii *36*

Chapter 5
Rewriting Our Mother/ Daughter Stories with Love By Tara Fries . . *48*

Chapter 6
The Script Rewritten By Caroline A. Janssens *54*

Chapter 7
Journey Home To Love By Patricia L. Lai *59*

Chapter 8
The spiraling pattern of healing By Heidi Zin *66*

Chapter 9
Legacy of a Life Lived in Love By Alli Nathan *76*

Chapter 10
My Two Mothers By Beatrice Andrade *86*

Chapter 11
A Legacy of Love: Breaking the Chain of Abuse By Shelley Whizin and Sarah Schultz *98*

Chapter 12
Changing My Early Agreements with Life By Christine Judal *109*

We are not our mothers, but we carry their legacy. The question is: What parts of that legacy will we carry forward, and what parts will we release?" – Cheryl Strayed

Foreword

Judy Wilkins-Smith

I love you/ I hate you healing the daughter-mother dynamic/wound.

I will begin the foreword by asking if you have listened to my Meditation on the Mother. I am not trying to scare you into buying it, but this constellations meditation allows you to view your mother differently and make life-changing choices.

We all look at our mothers as just that- our mothers. But your mother was once a child with her own mother. She, too, had a relationship with her own mother – good or bad, and that directly influenced her relationship with you for either good or bad.

The primary reason for hating our mothers is that we want so much to be loved by her. Imagine that? It's true and painful for those who don't have a mother who loves and cares for her daughter, but I'd like to show you why it's not quite as simple as you may think.

I also want you to become very aware that your relationship with your mother has absolutely nothing to do with her relationship with you. That's important. It takes you right out of feeling victimized by it, right there. Now, there's something you can do, and that's powerful. You don't have to sit with all of this sadness anymore. In fact – it probably doesn't belong to you in the first place, but you take care of it as though it did. So, just like Alice – let's examine that looking glass just a little closer.

It's important to be aware that relationships span generations, and all the unfinished patterns keep cycling down to the next in line, hoping that this will be the person to acknowledge what's there, give the pattern its place, and then create a new pattern of their own. Hello- that next person is you! You are it – the change agent, and so the pattern showed up precisely the way that it did in order for you to change it into something remarkable. You see, right at the pattern you like to call a wound or broken place or a place where you are stuck – is the magic. The pattern that's trying to emerge. The new pattern and, of course – the new emotional DNA.

For those readers who have no idea what emotional DNA is – it's your inherited patterns of thoughts, feelings, and actions. Yup, they didn't just pop up out of nowhere; they are either multigenerational patterns, or you started them. In either case, do you really want to pass these on to your children, communities, or the world? If you want to change the world, it begins right here. With your mother. Your first bond.

So, how do you inherit your emotional DNA? There are a few ways. Just like physical DNA, these patterns don't care whether you know about their origins or not. They exist. Unlike your physical DNA, there's actually a lot you can do about it. In fact, while the pattern began out there somewhere, the change all begins with you. No excuses, no astoundingly good reasons to hang onto your wounds and feelings., If you truly want change, you are going to have to be the change.

But back to the drawing board. How do these patterns begin? They begin with a triggering event – good or bad and the decisions we make about the event, in turn, lead to thoughts, feelings, and actions that become patterns that, in turn, become mindsets that then become the truth. Only it's not the truth. It's your truth, and you can change that anytime you want to.

So, the event happens to someone before you, which, in turn, creates a language that becomes the substance of – in this case, mother and daughter's relationships. Your great-grandmother loses the love of her life and must go to work to provide for her children. She has a lot of pain, and she also has no time to think about being the smiling-playing mother she was. Your grandmother cares for the younger ones but often feels her mother's impatience when she gets things wrong. She, in turn, never wants children because she feels the loss of her father and, in a large sense, her mother and doesn't want to sentence another child to that possibility. Along comes your mother, who is told she wasn't wanted but has no idea of the context of why and thinks it's her fault. (Don't we all?) that. She has no idea that her mother is as hurt as she is, and so the pattern repeats, and now there's you, and this truly precious pattern is in your hands. You see, once you begin to put the pieces together or even if you don't have the pieces – once you make the choice to change the pattern, the emotional DNA begins to change. In your hands)

7

It takes just one thought, feeling, and action at a time to begin changing the pattern into something new and special. Perhaps for the first time, you as a mother can look at your child through the eyes of joy and connection, and maybe you, as the daughter, granddaughter, or great-granddaughter, get to tell your ancestors: "For all of you who couldn't connect – I will. I will restore the connection and happiness that once flowed."

There is a second well-studied way to inherit these patterns—again, without knowing your ancestors: epigenetics, a complex emerging science that studies such patterns. Studies of the Great Dutch Hunger Winter, the Holocaust, and 9/11 all show the same evidence: Trauma can be and is inherited.

The science behind this is something I will leave to you to study in depth if you choose, but to put it simply, when an event happens with a sustained set of strong emotions, this creates an imprint on your genes that then affects gene expression. If the emotional DNA is inherited this way, it may also affect your health, wealth, and every aspect of your life. In this case, of course, it may affect the mother-daughter relationship. Perhaps you inherited an unhappy relationship with your mother and, along with it, all the stress and maybe even ill health that comes with that. Perhaps just like your ancestors or women you feel the burden or feel all alone. You are the one who can change that – and it's time that you did.

It's important for you to realize that you are the magician in your own world. When your brain tells your body a story that your body can believe, it becomes the new truth, and so the question becomes: "What new truth do you wish to create? What new mother-daughter relationships do you want to see in your family line? When you look at your daughter or other women in your community, how will you be the magician who awakens that in others?"

Your mother is the first bond that you have in your life. She is also the source of love, life, connection, the birth of opportunities, and business. So, if you are thinking about disowning her or rejecting her, it's not that it makes you a bad daughter. You are, however, shutting the doors to all the knowledge you need to do well in your life. You may struggle to connect with others or trust relationships. Your business may miscarry or be aborted.

The discipline of systemic work and constellations looks at these patterns so that they can stop. Emotional DNA looks at these patterns and asks: "What's more is possible? What is the purpose of this pattern? Where is the magic in this train wreck? How is it mine to use and to grow into the shining gift and strength it was meant to be?

If you are reading this book, you are already curious about what is possible. You will be reading about courageous women who have walked this path or are still on it. Transformation is not for the chosen few; it is for those who choose it.

And to those of you who say: "This work is too hard," I would ask, is it any harder than the commitment you make to yourself every day to struggle?

On the other side of what seems like brick walls are the relationships with mothers that perhaps you never dreamed were possible. They exist, and they are places where new relationships flourish.

Once upon a time, your mother was just a little girl, just like you. Perhaps she never had much kindness, or perhaps it got lost. Right now, it and your relationship are in your hands. It isn't yours to heal for the two of you; it's yours to heal for yourself. When your heart opens, you may find peace or even see your hand outstretched to a mother who couldn't give it.

I wish you all so much joy, so much laughter, and such rich and fulfilled relationships with your mothers. The change in the world begins with you and then with the two of you, and the story you write will touch us all.

About Judy Wilkins-Smith

Judy is a highly regarded international, organizational, individual, and family patterns expert, systemic coach, and trainer. Founder of the US company System Dynamics for Individuals & Organizations, she is a sought-after motivational and informational speaker for conferences and businesses.

Her credentials read like the Who's Who List of Corporate America. Just a few of her clients are NASA, Microsoft, Pfizer, Exxon Mobil, Shell, Chevron, JP Morgan, Kraft Heinz, MARS Petcare North America, MARS LATAM, and the William Morris Agency.

Passionate about individual human potential, visionary leadership, and positive, accelerated global change, Judy's work is truly revolutionary. Through her unique ability to understand critical relational dynamics and patterns in personal and organizational systems, she has taken Systemic Work and Constellations' highly esteemed healing methodologies to a whole new level for use as powerful new tools for personal growth and organizational transformation.

Introduction

By Betsy Chasse

A dear friend once told me, "If your daughter doesn't tell you she hates you at least once in her life, you aren't doing it right." Those words stayed with me, perhaps because they felt like both a strange comfort and a painful truth. I know for a fact that, on many occasions, I told my mother I hated her.

I have fond memories of my mother, but for a long time, I didn't think of her fondly. That changed when I began to unravel the generational narratives we'd both inherited—narratives passed down like heirlooms, with neither choice nor consent.

I was raised to be strong and independent, to count on no one but myself, while also being programmed to marry and have children—two expectations that don't often mix well. My early years followed that script. I married young, and my first marriage ended almost as quickly as it began. I was completely unprepared for the reality of being in a relationship, let alone a marriage. For a while, I thought I'd never try again. But by the time I was barely thirty, I found myself grappling with the conflicting belief that I should be able to do it all on my own while wondering, "Why am I not married?"

I remarried, but that marriage ended ten years later when I realized what I'd mistaken for love was, in truth, a form of self-abandonment. I had allowed myself to be diminished—through words and actions that reminded me I was never "enough" unless I had a man by my side. And yet, for some reason, the men always left.

It wasn't until my late forties that I began to uncover the deeper patterns shaping my life. Working with Judy Wilkins-Smith, we traced a thread back through generations of my family. A pattern emerged: the men always left. Sometimes by choice, sometimes by circumstance. My grandmother had multiple husbands, all of whom died unexpectedly, leaving her to raise children in a world where women weren't even allowed to open a bank account. Going back further, I saw the same story repeating itself—women left to shoulder extraordinary burdens, surviving in ways that defied their time.

I am the youngest of six children, with four older brothers and one sister, and from an early age, I carried the weight of my family. As a child actress, I became the breadwinner, the one responsible for how good Christmas would be, for my mother's mood, and for so much that a child should never have to bear. My father was a dreamer and, at least for me, not much of a disciplinarian. My mother took on the responsibility of keeping everything in order.

Yes, there were times I hated her—hated the choices she made, which often seemed more about my success as an actress than my growth as a child. But looking back, I now understand that my anger was never really about her. It was about the frustration of not understanding her story and not understanding why she made her choices.

This is the heart of the mother-daughter relationship. We don't hate our mothers; we just don't know how to handle the anger, rage, and frustration that arise when we don't understand them. But in their stories, we begin to find our own. Through understanding, we can start to forgive—not just them but ourselves.

The women who share their stories in this book are doing just that: breaking cycles, shifting narratives, and rewriting the generational scripts we've inherited. These are stories of healing, of transformation, and of courage.

Perhaps the idea that your child has to say "I hate you" for you to parent well is a myth—a story we tell ourselves so we can avoid the hard work of healing. What I've learned from my own children is that healing is possible. As I began to heal the generational wounds passed down to me, I saw my children transform. I saw myself evolve as a parent and as a person.

It's never too late to start the process of healing. And as the stories in this book will show you, healing doesn't just change your life—it transforms the generations that came before you and the generations yet to come.

About Betsy Chasse

Betsy Chasse is the founder and "Top Cat" at Rampant Feline Media, a multi-media company dedicated to sharing books, films, and, most importantly, stories of humans navigating the complexities of life—growing and evolving along the way. Betsy, an award-winning filmmaker and bestselling author, is best known for her work on the acclaimed films What the Bleep Do We Know?, Song of the New Earth, and Energy: The Ultimate Healer. She has also authored several impactful books, including Tipping Sacred Cows, Killing Buddha, and The Writer's Room.

Chapter 1

Hell On Heels: Nice Women Do Not Divorce

By Claudia Micco

The atmosphere in the courtroom was heavy, the kind of tension that makes your heart race and chest heavy. My grandmother, Helen, stood before the judge, her face lined with exhaustion, hands clenched tightly in front of her, and her fingernails digging into her skin in an attempt to hold herself together. She had her four children by her side—Audrey (8), Robert (7), Barbara (6), and Edwina, almost three. She spoke quietly but firmly, recounting years of abuse. Her husband, the defendant, had terrorized her for so long that the specifics blurred together, but one incident stood out. He had come home drunk again, violent as ever, and attacked her so viciously that she thought this time she might not survive.

She had gone to the police many times, hoping for protection, but nothing ever changed. After years of enduring his cruelty and holding onto hope that he would change, she made the decision that would alter the course of her life: she sought a divorce.

It was December 6, 1948. The winter was brutally cold that year, but the cold outside was nothing compared to what she had endured inside her own home. Helen asked the court for custody of her children, whom she had been raising almost entirely on her own. She also requested financial support and help with attorney fees. Tears filled her eyes as she pleaded for any relief the court could offer.

As I grew older, I learned that this day marked a turning point for my grandmother, a day of both loss and courage. She made the bold decision to leave a man who had terrorized her—a man I would never know. In fact, I didn't even learn of his existence until I was a teenager. By then, he had already passed away, and his name was a ghost in our family. My grandmother's strength, her will to survive and protect her children, pulled her through an abusive marriage at a time when women had few options. This was no small feat, especially when such actions were unheard of for a woman. Divorce was stigmatized during this period, and those who divorced faced social ostracism and severe judgment. Sadly, her story is not unique; it has been repeated countless times throughout history and continues to this day.

Growing up, my family had many secrets. I always thought of Grandpa Sam as my real grandfather. Sam, my grandmother's next husband, was the man who showed love and care for my grandmother and our family. Sam was a short and stocky man born of Sicilian immigrants. He was a chef at the iconic Bendix Diner, an old-fashioned stainless steel fixture on the median between Route 17 North and South in Hasbrouck Heights, New Jersey. Grandpa Sam treated my grandmother like a queen. He waited on her hand and foot. She never seemed to have to lift a finger. Our family joked that she had a magical power over him. All of my memories of him are warm and full of laughter. But after he passed away, I discovered that Sam wasn't my biological grandfather at all.

The truth came out slowly, first in whispers, then in stories shared after his death. He had always been a heavy smoker—Camel and Lucky Strike were his favorites—and he developed lung cancer in his early sixties. When he was diagnosed, the truth was kept from him, possibly out of love, fear, or both. He may have secretly known he was terminal, but I will never know. One afternoon, after returning from a doctor's appointment, he collapsed in his favorite gold Lazyboy chair, struggling to breathe. Blood filled his mouth as he coughed, and big red chunks started coming from his mouth. I ran to him, holding him as he slipped into unconsciousness. My grandmother was frantic, racing up and down the hallway, clutching the walls, and screaming for help. My parents heard them from the downstairs apartment and called an ambulance since we didn't have cell phones back then. The ambulance arrived, but by then, it was too late. He was gone. While the rest of the family rushed off to the hospital, I stayed behind to clean up the bloody mess on the living room floor. At 14, it was my first encounter with death in all its ugliness, nothing like what I had imagined it to be.

In the aftermath, I learned more about my grandmother's past and the secrets she had kept. Sam wasn't her legal husband, and the man I thought of as my grandfather had only been in her life after she escaped the unimaginable horrors of her first marriage. The man I thought was my loving, balding, Sicilian grandfather -who used to make me tuna fish sandwiches while I watched Felix The Cat- turned out to be my step-grandfather, and his death revealed a lot of things I never knew about him or my grandmother's past. It turned out that Helen and Sam were not legally married. They were living in "sin". Her real husband, Vincent, was a man she had married in 1938, just before the war, but their marriage was marked by violence almost from the start.

Vincent beat her while she was pregnant with their first and second child, accused her of infidelity, and belittled her every chance he got. His alcoholism fueled his cruelty, and even after she involved the police again in 1947, when he threatened to harm himself and her at knifepoint, nothing changed. For nearly a decade, she endured both physical and emotional torment.

Divorce in 1948 was not common, especially for women, and legal systems favored men. To leave, women had to prove their husband's cruelty, and even then, it wasn't guaranteed. My grandmother managed to find a lawyer willing to take her case, a rare and courageous act at the time. My grandmother, Helen, had a particularly difficult experience with her divorce. After her death, at age 94, I became the holder of the records and court documents from the 1940s, all of which were on carbon copies. I discovered that her husband had a mental illness, was an alcoholic, and was abusive towards her. Despite these struggles, she persevered in finding a lawyer to help her get a divorce, which was almost unheard of for a woman then. After her divorce, she was left alone to raise four young children, one of whom— my uncle—was a "forceps baby." Back then, the term used was "mentally retarded," as a result, and he was sent to live in a state institution in 1951. He struggled developmentally, and there were few options in those days. My grandmother had no help from the church or the community, and Vincent would abandon his children and the court-ordered duties to provide any assistance to their future care. She worked as a waitress to survive and took on any odd jobs she could find. In those days, it was common for struggling mothers to send their children to live with other families during the week. My mother and her sisters were placed with one such family, but instead of care, they were neglected and abused. Unknown to my grandmother at the time, but behind closed doors, this family did not provide basic hygiene for my mother and her sisters. They were forced to eat cucumber and tomato sandwiches and slept in the basement on makeshift beds made out of chairs pushed together.

The stories my mother eventually told me about this time were dark and difficult to comprehend. The man who cared for them was a predator, his sly smile hiding the twisted desires that he inflicted upon the girls in his care. They were subjected to unspeakable abuse, their innocence shattered and replaced with deep scars that never fully healed. My mother managed to escape the cycle of addiction and mental illness that consumed her siblings, but her sisters were not as fortunate. Her younger sister fell into drug addiction, her once bright mind clouded by the grip of substance abuse. She was diagnosed with paranoid schizophrenia in the 1960s and sent to Graystone, a famous mental institution, until it was abandoned, leaving her behind with only the echoing memories of her former self. She also left behind three young children, who were awarded to the state because my grandmother was not legally married. It was a devastating blow for my grandmother, watching helplessly as her grandchildren disappeared into the abyss of the social services system. She would never see them again. After a brief release, my aunt found herself unable to function on the outside due to her condition and spent the rest of her life in another mental hospital until she passed away. Her older sister was an artist and talented cook, but her life took a tragic turn when she married an abusive man. She turned to alcohol as a coping mechanism, ultimately succumbing to its destructive grasp at just 42 years old. My uncle, who struggled with developmental disabilities, remained in the New Lisbon Developmental Center until his death. Despite being separated by distance and circumstance, we visited him often throughout the years.

Even in the face of so much hardship, Helen refused to give up. After our beloved Grandpa Sam passed away, she returned to work as a waitress, determined to provide for herself again, now a much older and wiser woman. As I reflect on their relationship, I realize that my grandmother had found someone who was completely different from her first husband. Despite facing numerous challenges - losing both of her daughters to mental illness, recovering from an abusive marriage, and being a divorced woman - she remained determined and resilient. She found love once again later in life, marrying a man who adored her just as much as Grandpa Sam; though she ended up caring for him after a stroke left him incapacitated, they were very much in love.

"Helen Heels," as her friends called her for her stylish high-heeled shoes, was a woman of indomitable spirit, and for her time, she was also "Hell on Heels." Her story is one of survival, but it's also a testament to the quiet strength women of her generation had to muster just to make it through. The battles she fought—both in and out of the courtroom—are the legacy she left behind. Her resilience is in my blood, passed down through the generations, a thread of determination that runs through the women in our family.

Looking back now, I see my grandmother not only as a stylish woman who dressed to impress but as a symbol of endurance and persistence. Her life, marked by so much pain, is also one of triumph. She raised her children, buried her demons, and found a way to keep moving forward. That strength, more than anything, is what I carry with me. My grandmother was the embodiment of stoicism, strength, and quiet resilience. She raised the bar in handling challenges and never backed down. Growing up, I didn't fully realize her impact on me, but as I got older, I began to see her tenacity reflected in myself. My ability to break molds, defy expectations, and pursue things that were different or challenging clearly came from the genes I inherited from her. There's likely even a bit of her audacity and appetite for adventure in me—traits that sometimes lead me to trouble but also to growth.

Looking back on her life, I recognize how deeply she influenced our family, particularly in shaping us as strong, independent women who wouldn't tolerate disrespect. It took me years to understand that my hyper-independence was a legacy she passed down. It's a trait with both its benefits and drawbacks, but it set me on a path that challenged conventions, especially in my choice not to have children. While some may see this decision as complicated or burdensome, for me, it has become a way of owning my life and values. My grandmother's example of breaking societal norms—making choices when women were just beginning to gain such freedoms—showed me that it was possible to define my life on my own terms.

Even though I'm often questioned about my life choices, I carry my grandmother's wisdom. She would say, "Just do what you want, be happy, and don't listen to a man. But if you do, make sure it's one who takes care of you." Her advice and courage continue to guide me, empowering me to embrace my path without apology.

Claudia Micco is a wellness expert, author, and teacher trainer with over 40 years of experience in fitness and mind-body education. Based in Maui, she is the creator of HypnoFitness, integrating cognitive hypnosis with exercise for trauma recovery and stress management. Claudia has co-authored works like "50 and Fabulous" and "Lessons Learned the Hard Way" while presenting at global fitness conferences and training programs. As an ACE-certified educator, she specializes in trauma-sensitive fitness and mindfulness practices, empowering professionals and individuals worldwide.

Chapter 2

The Eyes Of An Old Mother

By Catherine Stilo

Her head peered around from behind the pole she had climbed to hide from me, and our eyes met. She turned away, shyly revealing her slightly distended belly and swollen nipples. In an instant, I completely understood. "I don't want your chickens, just their feed. I am nursing and doing it alone, so I need easy access to food to sustain myself." It was a Mama Raccoon that had scrambled from the feeder inside our coop out into the run when she sensed me coming. With the feeder swinging back and forth and the chickens safe outside, unsettled but unharmed, I knew this to be true. She was caring for many mouths and had no energy to search for food for herself. I could tell by the folds of her belly it was not her first litter; she had done this many times before. Her slow, heavy blink said it all - she was old and tired, and being a mother was hard.

The encounter stirred something deep and primal within me. Inked in my memory, I have replayed this profound moment several times over but didn't understand its significance or symbolism until now as I started reflecting on another mother, where seeing eye-to-eye has not come as swiftly or easily and almost never came at all.

My relationship with my mom has been extremely challenging, never having the type of connection for which I had hoped. Riddled with criticism, our relationship lacks closeness and is a constant battle of what I want versus what she thinks I should do. I never considered the other side of things or wondered about my mother's experience. Having been conditioned to believe that motherhood is the most natural thing, an expected progression in the life of every woman, I never considered that, in some respects, it could be hard.

Even though, from what I saw of motherhood growing up, it looked very hard, I am not sure why it took so long to realize that it could be. My own childhood consisted of constraint and control, and, to me, a mother was a source of demands, limitations, and opinions based on knowing what is best and what is considered "proper" behavior for a woman. It also seemed that having children meant sacrificing one's own desires for those of her family. My mother put her children before all else. She made her children her whole world, albeit a world in which there didn't seem to be any happiness. Seeming completely worn out and exasperated, I often remember evenings when she slumped her head down on her arms, sobbing, alone at our kitchen table.

Looking back, I can put the pieces together. My mom was an old mother having me, her first, at forty, unheard of in days when most people started families at twenty. Her fondest childhood memory was playing with her friends at "The Quarry," a rocky natural space in the neighborhood. Those close friends she had growing up fell away as they met their loves, married, and had kids early on. With very different lives and other priorities, they went their separate ways.

Why she didn't follow and marry when her friends did is unclear. She didn't enjoy her job as a nurse, so I can't imagine that was the reason. She has said that there was never a match; the ones she was interested in were never interested in her, but I have to consider that perhaps she really didn't want to, something you couldn't admit at that time. I remember one of her mantras: "[s]he travels fastest, who travels alone," meaning you can see and do more if you don't have to consider other people's needs. Another of her mantras, heard in moments of exasperation, was "Think twice before you say I do." Those two mantras likely illuminate the more truthful answer.

When she finally did marry, there was only a short biological window left, so she couldn't waste any time having children, or it would be too late. She had me not long after being wed, leaving only a few months of being a new couple before the journey of pregnancy and motherhood began. Her own friends, having long passed this stage, meant there would have been no one to talk with about what was happening, difficulties nursing, potty-training, or getting kids to eat.

Other mothers with kids the same age would have been ten or twenty years younger, so it must have been hard to relate. It was a time before information was one click away, before there were books on these topics, before Oprah or Dr. Phil, and before postpartum depression was even understood. Like Mama Raccoon, I imagine my mom felt very alone as a mother, but unlike her, being a mother didn't just happen as the natural order of things. Being a mother was a choice, though it may not have seemed like one in those days. Maybe unconsciously, it was a choice she felt conflicted about making, especially that late in life.

I discovered, as a teenager, that my mom lied to us about her age, claiming to be ten years younger than she actually was. One day, my brother asked innocently what year my dad was born and, being very sharp, quickly realized the math didn't work. At the time, I thought it was extremely odd and always wondered why she lied to us about something as innocuous as her age. I realize, now, that it wasn't innocuous. It compounded the already difficult role of being a mother and was a major factor contributing to the tension between us and our challenges in seeing eye-to-eye.

I couldn't appreciate my mother or the experiences that shaped her because I never realized the age gap was so wide or that it made such a difference in how we see things, especially when it comes to views about women. With forty years between us, she could have been my grandmother, and there was no buffer of a mother in between to bridge the uncommonly wide generation gap.

Born in the 1930s, my mom was a small, frail child and the youngest of ten children. Her father died two weeks after she was born, leaving her mother, my grandmother, to provide for a large family on her own. My grandmother had been brought over from Italy to a strange country to help a grieving man. She never wanted to come, but "they" told her she should, not because it would be good for my grandmother, but because there was a man who had lost two wives already, leaving six kids in need of a mother. I asked why my grandmother didn't just say no, and my mother's answer reveals an underlying conditioned belief that women in those days didn't have much of a choice.

Many of my mother's other underlying conditioned beliefs stem from the indoctrination of religious dogma. Church and school were big influences in her life, and because nuns taught school, the influence of the church doubled. The strict and rigid teachings of long ago filtered through to how I was raised under control, fear, suffering, and conservative views on appropriate behavior, dress, and activity. Passion of any kind was frowned upon, especially sexual passion. My mom had very distinct ideas about what a "proper" woman was and what it meant to be a lady, and constantly worried about what other people would think. This was a big area of a lot of our clashes.

I remember wanting to take dance lessons and not being allowed. I could, however, take piano lessons. I didn't understand this as a child. Clearly, it wasn't about having the money; otherwise, all lessons would have been out of the question. In hindsight, the piano was for a "proper lady" and something my mother wished she had studied. The freedom and access to the energy I would gain in moving my body in dance were too much for staunch Roman Catholic stigmas and ideas about where that would lead. After all, the body was dirty, sinful, and a thing to be covered up and hidden. She likely felt forbidden to access that freedom in her own being. Maybe my mom wanted to suppress my ability to access it in mine.

I also wasn't allowed to attend school dances or go on dates. Maybe she was trying to save me from marrying too soon. Maybe she wanted to prevent me from having what she hadn't been able to find: the love of my life. Maybe a little bit of both. I can't really know for certain, but I do know one explanation feels truer than another. Ironically, after being forbidden to date or even interact with boys during my formative years, my mom then wondered why, at thirty, I still wasn't married.

Years ago, when I started dating my current partner, the values clash of the generation gap reared its ugly head as we planned a trip together. When I told my mom, the excitement I expected was met, instead, with outrage and the question of why was I doing this to her. When I asked what was so upsetting, she revealed that she felt it was inappropriate for an unmarried woman to go on a trip with a man and tipped her hand to some belief that "I was going to hell, and it was her job to save my soul." I remember hating my mother for being so backward, and now think maybe she hated me for being so forward as to go against how women should behave according to her societal view of the feminine and for angering her fearsome god, who saw everything as sinful.

On that same thread, I was ambushed one Thanksgiving after my partner and I had been dating for a while. She pulled me aside with my dad and asked, "Don't you want to be happy? Don't you want to get married and have kids?" Her worldview, once again, shaped her words despite the fact that she was married and had kids and never really seemed all that happy. She went on to warn me that I would never be happy because he couldn't commit, that he didn't really love me, or he would marry me. He was just having his fun.

It took me years to unravel and sort through her implications. In fact, I am still working through it. I realize that instead of being able to see me as a successful, independent woman, all she could see was her failure as a mother and as a Roman Catholic. For her, it was a double whammy that, I only now understand, may have also been peppered with a hint of jealousy.

Maybe not getting married and having kids was an insult to her. Maybe, on some level, she felt it was because she didn't give a good enough example growing up to make me want to become a mother. She never asked me about not having kids, which I am sure is out of politeness, but it could also be because of fear of the answer. Layer on Catholic guilt, simply me living my own life triggered a belief that she was failing. Or maybe it triggered something else? Maybe in her own life, she could no longer hold out on the internal conflict about "what proper women did." Maybe someone ambushed her at Thanksgiving, and she succumbed to the pressure and finally gave in and wed. Maybe she was envious of the freedom that I, and all women, now had to make their own choices and live life on their own terms.

Even though my mother is still alive, it's hard, if not impossible, to find the answers. I have tried exploratory conversations, but when asked, her responses range from "Oh, I don't know" to "Oh, I don't remember" to flat-out denial of stories others have shared, saying "That's not true" and even going back on things she once told us. I attribute this to worldview and upbringing. She grew up in a time where feelings were not allowed or discussed, and niceties were valued over truthfulness, so I can only make suppositions and assumptions based on the understanding I have gained about the human condition.

As I reflect back, I see that I never allowed her any leeway, either. I clearly had a preconceived notion of what motherhood should be, look like, how a mother should behave, and how kids should be treated. I spent most of our relationship in blame, blaming her for falling short of my expectations. It didn't help that those expectations were likely created by the idealistic image of T.V. moms – June Cleaver and Carol Brady waltzing through life, always so put together and with the right words at exactly the right moments. I didn't take into consideration that being a real mother, not a T.V. one, may not have come naturally or easily and that it actually might be quite hard. I also am just realizing that it is a two-way street, a dance, and maybe our relationship never became what she hoped it would be, either.

Unimpressed by the expression of depressed helplessness and smothering overprotectiveness I saw in my mother, I was determined to become the exact opposite – a career-driven, cosmopolitan, liberated woman with a life of parties, drinking, fun, and wild adventures. In hindsight, I realized I hated being a woman and being associated with what I felt were "weaker" traits so much that I swung the pendulum to the other extreme. To be perceived as a "strong woman," I closed my heart, shut down all feeling, compassion, and empathy in favor of power. If I hadn't, I would have understood the other side of my mother's story and that she may have been conflicted about her choice to become one.

It is with greater understanding that I go into relationship with my mother. I have to accept that there is a high probability she didn't want to get married and have kids, but that's what you did in her day. Women didn't have much of a choice. She likely envied me and the freedoms that I was enjoying as a woman. I always felt that my mother had unfair expectations for me, wanted me to be someone I wasn't, and wanted me to be a carbon copy, a "mini-her." I realize I had some, too. I had expectations that were unfair to her. I wanted her to be someone she wasn't and couldn't be instead of letting her be the mother she was. Maybe she wanted to be someone else, too, which explains why she lied about her age and behaved as she did. I certainly wanted to be someone else hiding behind a persona of power.

Who I am today has everything to do with my relationship with her. I am the product of all her experiences, whether by repeating the same patterns, rebelling against them, or some combination of both. Like it or not, her life is the life on which mine is built. I am not fated by this fact but liberated by it through understanding its influence. It's not preventing me from being but presenting me with an opportunity to overcome.

We can only respond to life in a way that was modeled for us. Mothers are doing the best they can from what they know, balancing conditioning and expectations with the desires of the heart. My mother was doing that. Animal mothers follow natural order, teaching their offspring how to survive on their own and how to find food and water. Human mothers have the added complexity of choosing to become a mother and then teaching their babies how to thrive. Some of us are born into functional models, and some are born into dysfunctional models, making life easier or more challenging depending on where we go with it.

Relationships are complex. There are many layers and many versions of the stories we tell ourselves about them, depending on which lenses we are using. This is only one version of the one I have with my mother, which is simplified to try to make sense of it. I can't control what my mother thinks or how she acts, but what I can control is the story I make from it and my actions that follow. I can stop pointing fingers in blame and instead turn that light back on myself to illuminate what beliefs in me still need to be examined.

I have realized that relationships are neither painful nor pleasurable; they simply are. Pain comes when I try to control things, to push and pull them in the direction I want. I am learning not to impose my will on others, to release expectations and love them for who they are, not who I want them to be. I don't know what they've been through or what experiences have colored their worldviews, and I look closely at the ones that have colored mine. I don't know what armor is around a person's heart because I am, only now, discovering the armor that is around mine.

While understanding came in a flash in that exchange with Mama Raccoon, it took a lifetime with my mother. We may be more alike than I thought. Although we probably never will see eye-to-eye, I have learned to see heart-to-heart. Our eyes are of different generations, one deeply rooted in the past and one envisioning the future, but our hearts rest in the present moment. When we come to it without expectation, just allowing, only then, can we be liberated. This moment ripples back and out in healing and hope. Changing the present changes the past and allows a connection to all mothers and all daughters in a new way.

About Catherine Stilo

Drawing from over three decades of personal practice and certifications in movement, intuitive development, and nature connection, Catherine is a creative facilitator blending sensory awareness with the art of story and the wisdom of the natural world.

With her partner, John, she co-created Terra Kula, a permaculture orchard of over three hundred fruit tree guilds on an acre and a half to demonstrate the possibilities for abundance.

Her mission is to know and share the magic of feeling wildly alive, fully embodied, and living a more authentic, connected life. Most often, you'll find her barefoot in the grass, flowing with harmonious, alive, and "unplugged" vibes.

Visit TerraKula.org to find out more about her ongoing adventures and upcoming workshops.

Chapter 3

Oh, The Tangled Webs We Weave!

By Dr. Theresa L. Smith, D.C.

I don't know about you, but as the years go by, I see things with so much more clarity. It truly makes my brain hurt to look back and try to understand the brainwashing that has been going on for centuries. How long has it been like this? Was it always this way? They always say hindsight is 20/20, but I don't see anyone really changing anything. I see the subservience women have been forced to live out—the hiding, the need to be who you aren't. The pain, the disgust, and the worthlessness passed from generation to generation. If this happened with all the women in my family, what about other families? Where did it start? It must have been long before the generations I know.

For me, everything started with my beautiful Grandma. She had the most delicate hands, adorned with beautiful rings, always dressed in style. Gloves, hats, stockings, and high heels—especially her high heels—were her signature. No matter what life threw her way, if you asked her, she was always "fine." Everything was always just fine.

I don't know how she managed it. Now, having lived much of my own life, I know that not everything is always fine. Yet, like her, I learned the lesson early: never show how you truly feel because that would be "wrong." It's exhausting pretending everything is perfect when it isn't. It requires stuffing down emotions and lying to yourself. It's preposterous and harmful.

Yet, that was how it was and continues to be.

I loved watching Grandma and helping her. She was a remarkably talented woman, though, "in her time," her skills were seen as nothing extraordinary. Every woman, it seemed, was expected to know how to sew, quilt, crochet, cook, clean, and be an impeccable hostess. Didn't all women strive to do that? Grandma sewed many of my clothes until I learned to do it myself. She made beautiful things—quilts and wall hangings I still treasure to this day. Her craftsmanship was a reflection of her care.

In her quiet presence, I found comfort. She was always there for me, listening, spending time, and making clothes. We baked together bread, pies, and my favorite—peanut brittle. She was so patient with me while making it, trusting me with the tricky task of pouring the hot brittle, which could easily burn us. Somehow, we never did.

Grandma also taught me to love gardening, sharing her knowledge of plants and flowers. She had an eye for beauty, which extended to how she set her table—fine china, crystal, and silver, always perfectly placed. She insisted everyone eat until they were full, and no one ever left hungry. She was a gentlewoman; I never saw her angry. At most, she'd mutter, "Oh, thunder," and that was it. No yelling, no fury—just quiet composure.

When I was growing up, Grandma was a minister's wife, a role she fulfilled with grace. The house was always spotless, the yard full of beautiful flowers, and she tended her beloved rose garden with care. It was a time when women wore hats to church and ironed sheets and their husbands' handkerchiefs. Everything had to be "perfect."

How did she become this woman? Grandma came to California as a young girl, all the way from Maine. She told me her father, Roscoe, was strict, and she was teased by other children for her clothes, which were different from theirs. Her mother passed before I could meet her, but I knew Roscoe, my great-grandfather, though only briefly. Grandma married young, eloping with my grandfather against her father's wishes. When my grandfather died suddenly of a heart attack at 40, Grandma was left alone with two children—my mother, who was 15, and my uncle, just 5. She had never worked before and suddenly had to find a job at a time when single mothers had no rights to credit or even renting a house.

29

Grandma found work at Bullocks, a high-end store in Pasadena, and later became a school secretary. I don't know how she met the man who would become the only grandfather I knew, but she remarried and became the quintessential minister's wife, hosting elegant gatherings and keeping everything just so.

She adored my uncle, her son, who was ten years younger than my mother. After my mom married and left home, Grandma poured all her attention into him, even when his struggles with alcoholism became evident. She couldn't—or wouldn't—see his faults, and it hurt my mother and others in the family. But that was how things were—families, especially women, held everything together with grace, even when it meant turning a blind eye.

Grandma told me things no one else did. We talked about everything, even topics like masturbation, which I never dared discuss with my mother. She encouraged me never to be afraid, assuring me that things always worked out. Her calm in the face of everything, even an earthquake, amazed me. I ran to her in a panic one night when the ground shook, but she lay in bed, unconcerned. "Why worry?" she said. "There's nothing to fear."

Despite being taught all the "proper" things for a woman of her time—piano playing, handwork, cooking, cleaning—Grandma had a rebellious streak. After my grandfather passed, she began her daily "tea"—which was really wine. We'd go to lunch and enjoy margaritas, and she loved getting tipsy. On Christmas mornings, mimosas became part of the tradition. I imagine she found ways to fit this little rebellion into her otherwise "perfect" minister's wife role.

Grandma also had a "list." At some point, everyone was on it. You wouldn't know why; you'd just feel the coldness in her demeanor. But as quickly as you found yourself on her list, you'd find yourself off it again. It was, I believe, her way of dealing with hurt while still maintaining the appearance of being "fine."

She lived to be 101, almost 102, and I am thankful for every lesson she taught me. While she wasn't perfect, she was my Grandma, and I loved her deeply.

Then there's my Mom. Mom was always seen as a lovely, kind, thoughtful woman. And she was, most of the time. However, after years of stuffing down emotions, she became quite adept at cutting you up with her tongue. Mom had a painful life. She lost her dad on her birthday at age 15. She lost my sister. She married a man who had other desires in life. She was a very depressed person. She cried at the drop of a pin. My Mom worked hard on quietly living life, doing what she was "supposed to," and stuffing all the emotions down. I rarely saw her happy—truly happy.

She always worked hard and tried to be a dutiful wife, cook, and entertain. She went to church. She was almost the perfect picture of subservience, except deep down, she was boiling over. She and my Dad always fought. He didn't appreciate her lack of organization, her cluttered home. And this never changed. She always had piles of stuff—everywhere. Of course, they could have fought about other things I didn't know about, but this was the most common disagreement.

Mom enjoyed cars. She had even taken a mechanics course, and she loved going to the races. I don't remember her taking me, but I must have inherited my love for cars from her. Mom didn't like to garden. She was an avid reader and studied the "Scriptures" most of her life. Her library of self-help books, Bibles, and theology studies was extensive. She also enjoyed embroidery and crocheting.

I'm sure part of her depression and anger was linked to my sister's passing. She died when she was four, and I was five. Mom would have been 23 years old. I can only imagine the guilt she carried, feeling responsible for something beyond her control. My sister died of spinal meningitis, and although we shared a room, I didn't get sick. I was passed off to relatives during the funeral, and I didn't attend. I have no memory of my sister, despite efforts to recover it. It's a void.

There were other reasons for Mom's depression. She had married a man who wasn't faithful—my Dad had other desires in life. And in those days, you didn't divorce. A woman couldn't survive without a man—she couldn't rent a house, get a credit card, or buy a car. Total control. Which is ridiculous to me. Religion didn't approve of divorce either. You were supposed to suffer through it and hope for the best.

Mom and Grandma had issues, although Grandma would never admit it. Mom stressed over it most of her life. She always felt Grandma favored her son and treated him better. There was even a time they didn't speak, though I don't remember why. Mom held onto those things, held onto everything.

Mom lived with constant pain—back pain. She had surgeries, rods, screws, and all kinds of prescriptions and epidurals, but nothing really helped. Counseling didn't help either. It wasn't until I learned about different healing modalities that she experienced breakthroughs, though it was never enough to fully free my Mom. This also fueled me to become the healer I am today...

In front of others, Mom was always "fine." Just fine. She tried to instill this in me, but I couldn't hold it in. I always talked about how I felt, trying to figure out what it all meant and what to do with it.

I'm actually grateful now that my parents weren't fully available to me. They had a lot of issues—issues I knew nothing about until later in life.

Then there was my Dad's sister, my Aunt Lee. She was a wild one! She smoked two packs a day, drank a fifth of liquor, and hung out in bars. She cussed, went out with all kinds of men, and lived her life completely differently from my Grandma and Mom. I got to live with her for a bit, and it was eye-opening. People judged her harshly, but she didn't care. She lived life on her own terms, slept with whoever she wanted, drank whatever she wanted. And while I wouldn't recommend her lifestyle, at least she was living it her way, free of society's expectations.

I don't know how my Grandma and my Mom kept quiet. I don't know how they survived. It's 2024 now, and when I was growing up, women couldn't buy or rent a house, especially with children. Credit was denied to women. Women had to exist with whatever man they had in their lives. There wasn't much choice back in the day as we do live in a patriarchal society, and keeping women subservient makes men's lives easier.

My parents weren't really available for me, so I raised myself. I remember calling my mom once when I had the German measles. I was so uncomfortable with the itching and wanted her to come home, but she didn't. Work was more important. Maybe that's why I loved my Grandma so much. She paid attention to me. She talked to me. And even though I became rebellious as I got older, she supported me, as did the only Grandpa I ever knew.

I have no idea where I got my courage to do new things. I sure wasn't raised around it. I am sure seeing that everyone was fine when they weren't, I must have decided to search for the truth, question everything, and ignore what they had taught me. To be quiet, to be fine. That was obviously not a good way to live. It wasn't until Aunt Lee came along that I could relate to anyone in my family. I started rebelling in my teens, like most teenagers. But unlike most, I kept going. I started asking questions. I was raised in a Christian school and went to church on Sundays and Wednesday evenings at Christian camps. I was surrounded by it, brainwashed by it. In high school, I began to question everything. I still do.

When I went to community college, classes like anthropology and philosophy shook everything I had been taught. Anthropology completely contradicted what the church taught. Philosophy gave me a headache—it was a totally new world of ideas that I had never been exposed to. The church is careful not to teach things that will make you think critically. They want you to follow without question.

Because of my rebellious streak, I often took paths that were harder than necessary. But it's led me here. I've lived a full life and experienced more than I would have if I'd just gone along with the idea that "everything is fine." Because it isn't, and if everything were fine, we wouldn't grow. We wouldn't learn. I don't think we're meant to go through life with everything just fine.

My daughter is a miracle. I wasn't supposed to be able to have children, but when I was 31, she came into my world. She's a person who sees through people quickly, speaks her mind, and lives life the way she sees fit. No, her life hasn't always been perfect, but I'm so proud of her. She's her own person—speaking her mind, sharing her soul, and her love. And my daughter has my Grandma's hands...

When I became a mother, I didn't want to raise my daughter the way I had been raised. I wanted her to have everything I never had and more. I wanted her to speak her mind—kindly, but speak it nonetheless. I wanted her to see people for who they truly are. I believed in truth, no matter how hard it might be. Speak it kindly, but don't hold back. Life is too short to be anything but real about what's happening.

This all leads me to the love I have for my Grandma, my Mom, and my daughter. And for myself. I love them for who they were and are. But I also hate them in a way—hate them because they lived a life of subservience, leaving me to break the cycle and change things. Women are so much more than playing piano, doing crafts, cooking, cleaning, and looking pretty. We are nurturers, behind-the-scenes warriors, the ones who kiss the boo-boos and support men while they blunder about. It's time to stand in our power, to speak out loud, to no longer accept the leftovers handed to us. The more of us that do this, the more strength we'll have.

I have pushed beyond the boundaries set by my ancestors, never fully understanding how or why I did it. I still don't understand the drive behind it, only that I did it. And now, I see things with more clarity, allowing me to be more intentional. I see where all the brainwashing and training came from. Before them, there was my Grandma and my Mom—they tried to continue it with me. And I'm working to break free, just as my daughter is, from the societal conditioning that says we should be less than.

Thankfully, I went out and found the information I needed to rewire my brain to come from a place of power. The conscious mind is so limited. We should all be taught how the brain works—the conscious, subconscious, and superconscious mind. Once you know how to operate them, you can manifest your desires. You can live the life you want. Not only will you love your life, your body will be healthier. Everything we think and feel goes into our bodies. We create health or dis-ease because all the issues are in the tissues.

The webs we weave entangle us into lives we don't want to live, forcing us to be what others want us to be. Struggling to untangle these webs is a lifelong challenge. The beliefs we were taught are deeply ingrained. They were deeply ingrained in our ancestors as well, so it's no wonder we've inherited them. Each generation struggles with the same entanglement. I still do, and I know my daughter does as well. The hope is that the next generation will do better than ours, better than our parents' and grandparents' generations. But instead, I see more of the same, just packaged differently.

Let's evolve. Let's break free. I choose to live a life of peace, joy, happiness, and abundance. What do you choose? Because whatever you choose is adding to the collective consciousness. I'd love to see the collective consciousness move toward a place of unconditional love, learning, and understanding. Let's make the world a better place. Shall we?

About Dr. Theresa Smith, D.C.

My interest in the healing arts began when I was in my 20s. I took courses in reflexology and massage. However, I had a career in business and family plans to settle down. I thought I knew where I was going. Life changed, and I was inspired to take my interest in the healing arts further to become a chiropractor. It took me ten years to realize my dream to help others through chiropractic care and other healing modalities as I worked full-time and parented my child as a single mother. I opened my first office in Sierra Madre and then moved to Monrovia 15 years later. Today, I offer Spinal Flow which assists the body to heal itself. It's a unique approach to health care that, in my own experience, has provided long-lasting and life-changing effects. Scientific research shows a clear link between what you think and how you feel, which affects your physiology and life. I also have a coaching program that will give you the tools to manifest your desires, find your true desires, rewire your thought patterns, and improve your health and life. Go to my website for more info: www.drtheresasmith.com. Feel free to contact me for any questions.

Chapter 4

Echoes of an Undreamt Life

By Karen Emi Fujii

Leave no dreams unfulfilled and cast aside,
Dwell not on all that was or could have been,
Hard is the heart that always is denied,
And closed to callings buried deep within.

I recently asked my now 91-year-old mother, "What were your dreams as a child?" There was a long and awkward silence as she struggled with a response. I tried to prompt her by rephrasing the question in different ways, but she was unable to articulate what possibilities, if any, she might have envisioned for herself.

Afterward, I was struck with the realization that a deep subconscious wound has been embedded in my maternal lineage. I have carried this same wound for much of my life as well.

I am the great-granddaughter of immigrants who made the arduous shipbound journey from Japan to the Territory of Hawaii in the 1800s. As my great-grandparents spoke little English, their children bore the primary responsibility for financially supporting the family.

My mother was born on the island of Hawaii in 1933. She grew up in a working-class family. Her father was the foreman of a coffee mill, and her mother was a domestic worker.

Their family lived in a simple home, with the main living area on one level and a basement for her father's workshop, where he made some of their household furnishings. The house lacked modern-day conveniences, such as indoor plumbing. Instead, they used an outhouse and relied on a water tank for their daily cooking and cleaning needs.

My mother has fond recollections of her childhood in Hawaii. An unmistakable sense of joy permeates her being when she talks about it. There seemed to be a simplicity and playfulness during those early years. She and her siblings enjoyed plenty of outdoor time with neighboring children. She delightfully recalls running foot races with the boys…and winning! Her family did not have many material things. So, they had to be resourceful, creating crude handmade toys from whatever materials were readily available. They even made play "shoes" using empty tuna cans, which they fastened to their feet by applying a sticky substance collected from a native pod.

My mother was eight years old when Pearl Harbor was attacked. Even now, she distinctly recalls specific details of that fateful December morning. She and her older sister were at church in Kona when their mother arrived unexpectedly at 8 o'clock with news of the bombing. She told them that they had to go home. My mother has never expressed much about the impact of that defining event or its aftereffects. When she speaks about that period, her voice has a subdued, matter-of-fact tone. In her sharing of the racial slurs directed towards the Japanese residents, including her and her family, there seemed to be a detached recounting of these incidents.

After graduating from high school, my mother attended Honolulu Business College, where she received a diploma in General Studies. She then worked for a local business until she married my father at age 33.

Around the time that my mother started working, her father was injured in a frightening accident at the coffee mill. As she recalls, he was adjusting the conveyor belt of a large coffee grinder when his shirt sleeve got caught in the belt. On the downturn, he was slammed to the floor. Her father sustained a head injury and remained unconscious for ten days in a local hospital. Although her father eventually returned home, he suffered some memory loss and remained permanently disabled.

My mother is the middle child of four siblings (two sisters and two brothers). While she and her younger sister remained at home with their parents, her older sister and brothers ventured out into the world. Her brothers attained undergraduate degrees and created lives away from Hawaii. My mother helped her younger brother with his college expenses because of their father's work-related injury. From her small paychecks, she would send monthly allowances of $600 to her brother.

My parents' first meeting was quite by happenstance. My mother, her mother, and my father's aunt were traveling on the same epic 40-day tour across North America. One of the cities on the tour's itinerary was Washington, D.C., where my father was working as a research chemist for a naval facility. During the tour's stop there, he met his aunt, who introduced them.

Following that brief encounter, my parents began a charming long-distance correspondence, exchanging handwritten letters between Honolulu and Washington, D.C. They eventually became engaged. After marrying, my mother relocated to the East Coast. They bought their first and only home in southern Maryland, where my younger sister and I were raised. After their marriage, my mother never worked. Typical for women of her generation, she became a dedicated homemaker and stay-at-home parent.

Throughout my life, there has been a familial emphasis on security and stability. I internalized these beliefs such that I became fearful of unknown situations. I developed an intense need for certainty. And I did not take unnecessary risks.

My family has also modeled the need to be self-reliant. On many occasions, my mother has been hesitant to ask for help because such requests might inconvenience others. Similarly, I have struggled with actively seeking support, especially emotional support.

Perhaps most significantly, there has been an undercurrent of emotional distance and detachment within my mother's family and between my mother and me. Some of this detachment reflects a culture that tends to be stoic and reserved. This is not to say that I was unloved. But, there was an absence of open expression of emotions, physical affection, and discussion of difficult life situations.

As a child, I was free to explore my imagination. And, the world seemed full of wondrous possibilities.

But, as often happens when those dreams are not nurtured, they become dormant and unrealized.

Beyond unmet basic emotional needs, I received no intentional encouragement to identify and express my own deep desires. There were no heartfelt conversations about my personal happiness. Subconsciously, I believed that it wasn't ok to have bold dreams. Instead, I developed a resigned acceptance of life circumstances.

This bleak perspective would become my embodied reality after a life-defining moment. As a teenager, I witnessed the dramatic decline in my father's health. He was diagnosed with congestive heart failure, ultimately resulting in his hospitalization. While hospitalized, he slipped into a comatose state from which he never regained consciousness. My mother made the difficult decision to remove him from life-sustaining machines. My father passed away at the age of 53, about a month after my 16th birthday. From that point forward, my life became a struggle, with an underlying pervasive heaviness and very few fleeting moments of pure joy.

This traumatic event had profound impacts into adulthood. After my father's death, I really had no support to process my grief. There was no open discussion within my family about what we were experiencing emotionally. So, I shut down. I shifted into survival mode. I disengaged from life. I withdrew into myself…and closed my heart.

My sense of security had been shaken to the core, and the internalized emphasis on safety and stability that has been ever-present in my maternal lineage was reinforced and strengthened.

I lost my belief in possibilities. I tried to do the responsible and "right" things. I resigned myself to following a certain path…one that was predictable and safe.

My life became a running checklist. I accumulated significant accomplishments, but there was no deep meaning for me.

I graduated from an academically rigorous science and technology high school with an exceptional GPA. Check.

I completed not one but two bachelor's degrees, graduating with high honors. Check.

I received a master's degree in Epidemiology from the top, most prestigious school of public health. Check.

I found stable employment in professional positions with respected public health organizations. I was financially secure, independent, and self-sufficient—check, check, and check.

I had attained everything that defined external success by societal, cultural, and familial standards. But, in doing so, I had unknowingly sacrificed my happiness and sense of self.

I was so focused on meeting these external expectations that I became disconnected from my authentic self. Instead of listening to my heart and intuitive knowing, I navigated life more and more from my head. I was not open to hearing my Soul's voice because I was always doing rather than being.

At a point in my life when I should have been thriving, I became lost and numb, jumping from job to job without a sense of purpose or direction. I was going through the motions of living rather than actively experiencing and engaging. I had no deep friendships or romantic relationships. I only revealed so much of myself to others. From the outside, I appeared to be fine, but internally, I was a chaotic mess and deeply suffering.

My soul was starving…for love, connection, and meaning.

A profound experience was needed to prompt my transformative journey and questioning of these norms and expectations because a fundamental shift within myself and how I viewed my world had to occur. But this journey really did not begin until I emerged from a very long and dark period.

Let not the heart be bound by unseen strings,
But set it free to soar to unknown heights,
And realize the peace such freedom brings,
From heavy heart oppressed by inner fights.

After several years of living independently, I moved back to my childhood home, mostly because I felt very isolated and lonely. I had no significant social connections or activities outside of work. Also, there was an underlying and increasing sense of responsibility for my aging mother. During those years away from home, I had been driving back and forth between my apartments and my mother's house quite frequently - every or every other weekend.

Upon my return, I was confronted with the harsh reality that my cherished home had changed dramatically. It barely resembled the home that I held in my childhood memory. Following my father's death, my mother bore an immense responsibility that broke her spirit in some sense. Over the ensuing years, there was a slow and steady decline in my mother's physical, mental, and emotional health. This decline was reflected starkly in the deterioration of our home's physical environment, both its internal and external spaces.

The yard, once lush and green and the envy of our neighborhood, had become overgrown and barren. The gardens, once overflowing with an abundance of flowers and vegetables, were now empty. The house itself was in obvious disrepair. Paint was cracked and chipping. Sections of the wooden window frames and sills were rotting. The original linoleum kitchen floor and living room carpet were worn and dingy.

With the absence of my father, it was no longer the orderly and pristine home of my childhood.

Inside, there was excessive clutter throughout the house. Piles of papers lay everywhere, covering the dining room and kitchen tables. Stacks upon stacks of things engulfed the available floor space in nearly every room. Innumerable purchases, many brand new and unopened, accumulated in the basement area. Excessive amounts of household supplies were scattered throughout the house. The refrigerator and freezer were stuffed with food items, many past their expiration dates.

I would try to discard things, but it was a never-ending and maddening endeavor. I would discreetly place things in the outside trash bin, only to be met with my mother's consternation.

It reached a low point when I discovered rotting produce (to the point of actual liquefication!) in grocery bags buried underneath piles in the kitchen and forgotten by my mother.

I would become so exasperated about our living conditions that the only way to communicate my frustration was by yelling, sometimes uncontrollably. During these desperate outbursts, my mother would stare blankly at me and/or respond in kind with hurtful comments.

In retrospect, I sense that the accumulation of these things gave my mother the security and control that had been shaken with the loss of my father. They seemed to serve as some sort of protective wall around her. But the clutter was suffocating me. The only sanctuary for me became my small childhood bedroom.

I felt growing frustration and resentment towards my mother because of her seeming indifference to my emotional pain.

Then, there was a spark of awareness within me. I cannot pinpoint the exact timing. It began as the emergence of an inner discontent that intensified into silent desperation with profound feelings of emptiness, loneliness, and sadness. I was in deep pain.

I felt like a ghost in this world. Silent and unseen. Existing, but not living.

I no longer wanted to experience this limited version of my life. I had a deep longing for something more.

After decades on such a narrowly defined path, I felt trapped in a deep chasm, without clarity about how to free myself.

Even though I was desperately unhappy, an intense fear of venturing into the unknown kept me tethered to situations and environments that were harmful in so many ways yet felt safe and familiar. The obsessive need to plan and know every detail of my life has been exhausting and kept me in a constant state of anxiety.

I did not know how to shift out of this state of being. Initially, I tried to strategize change with my mind, using an analytical approach based on my scientific education and experience.

I began to work with an established career coach for professional women. From our very early sessions, it was evident that deep inner work was needed.

I eventually gravitated toward this internal inquiry. I engaged in therapy, coaching, mindfulness practices, energy work, and self-growth groups. I would make some progress but could not sustain forward momentum. All of those inner monsters, in the form of deeply engrained beliefs and fears, continually resurfaced.

I was trapped in my mind and all of its rationalizations. I ignored those deeper yearnings. I wasn't ready to commit…to making a significant shift. I didn't yet have the faith and trust to take the leap, even though my life, as it was, was not working. I needed a big push from the Universe.

As I continued to ignore the whisperings of my heart, those messages became louder and the dissonance greater. I wasn't listening to these inner prompts, so the Universe, in its infinite wisdom, presented me with crises to nudge me into action.

Decisions rest upon the mind of one;
The path one takes if guided by one's heart,
Brings happiness when all is said and done,
And peace of mind from which one never parts.

THE pivotal moment presented itself in 2020. In the midst of the COVID-19 pandemic, several major life stressors converged simultaneously. I was working in public health, with direct involvement in COVID-response efforts, under intense conditions. My elderly mother transitioned unexpectedly from living independently to an assisted living situation. So, I was suddenly in a position of primary responsibility for managing her affairs, including the eventual sale of our family home, which forced me to uproot myself, relocating to be near work and family.

I became utterly depleted on all levels - physically, mentally, and emotionally. These were my darkest moments, during which I could not see a way forward. Feeling alone, empty, and lost, I was operating in pure survival mode.

I remember moments of profound sadness and desperately yearning for a more joyful and full life with love, connection, and purpose. I had a deep fear that I would never experience these things.

A fierce battle was waging within me between the inertia of what was safe and known and the pull of my Soul.

It was during this chaotic period that something miraculous happened. The personal upheaval experienced during the COVID-19 pandemic offered the gift of freedom from what had become an unbearable, lifeless existence for me…and my mother.

With her transition to a more supportive living situation, some of that childhood innocence has reawakened in my mother. I see the playfulness, and even joy, in her new friendships when they are engaged in lighthearted conversation or group activities, especially when they are immersed in their favorite game.

I experienced a tremendous shift and a deeper commitment to myself and to my growth and transformation. The most significant breakthroughs occurred not by trying to figure things out with my mind, as I had always done, but by turning inward and doing the things that frightened me the most… sitting in silence with myself…feeling my feelings…and really listening to my intuition and the callings of my Soul.

As I did so, I found a deep inner peace and felt more grounded than at any other time in my life. I started a daily meditation practice… I reconnected with nature…and I opened myself to receive the support of like-minded souls. And, most significantly, I began to take meaningful steps, small as they were, towards manifesting those callings.

To break from this cycle of retreating to safe and familiar situations, I had to step out of the self-imposed cage in which I had been confined for so long. I had to venture beyond my comfort zone and do things that challenged my sense of security.

When I allowed myself to be vulnerable and express more of my authentic self, the Universe responded with beautiful heart-centered friendships that seemingly entered my life at the precise moments when I most needed such support.

As my heart opened to the greater possibilities for my life, more beautiful synchronicities occurred.

Within one year, I manifested amazing soul-nourishing experiences, including two separate trips to Southeast Asia.

Upon reflection, I recognize a throughline of precious and powerful gifts within my maternal lineage. I am eternally grateful for the inner strength and resilience that have been passed down through my maternal ancestors to me.

These qualities are evident in my great-grandparents' journey from Japan and their personal stories of establishing and rebuilding their lives in a new and unfamiliar environment.

These same traits were embodied by my mother after my father's untimely death, as she navigated new responsibilities of single-handedly raising two young children and managing household affairs and finances.

I, myself, have sourced this deep well of strength and resilience during my most difficult life moments. These qualities have helped me to move through the darkness. And I know, with undeniable certainty, that these same gifts will empower me to step boldly into the next phase of my life.

So, where am I now? Still on my journey. More present and alive. Ever hopeful.

I am leaning into a more authentic way of being in this world, with openness and vulnerability.

I am courageously walking a transformative path of self-discovery, probably not traveled by anyone in my female lineage.

In doing so, perhaps I am realizing the unfulfilled wishes and dreams of my ancestors, who were unable to answer that calling in their hearts, and especially for my mother, who was never able to fully express that part of herself.

As I write these words, I feel greater empathy awaken within me. With compassionate eyes, I now see that my mother was bound by unspoken, deeply ingrained expectations for her entire life. These expectations did not afford the freedom to explore possibilities beyond her immediate circumstances. There was a sense of obligation to family and others before herself. Always tending to the needs of others, she was unable to dream for herself. Because my mother could not imagine the greater possibilities for herself, she could not verbalize these ideas to me. She did not have the language to do so. My mother was unable to communicate on a deeper level, from her heart, because she was not taught this type of communication. So, for most of my life, I could not envision the beautiful possibilities for myself.

By giving voice to what has been buried for so long, and as I embrace my life and dreams, I sense a profound healing of my female ancestral line.

True happiness cannot be based on this
Remorse for choices made and chances missed.

About Karen Emi Fujii

Karen Emi Fujii is an emerging author who, for nearly two decades, followed a safe and predictable path as a dedicated public health professional with state and local governmental agencies. By external standards, she should have been flourishing. Yet, beneath the surface, whispers of discontent grew increasingly louder until they could not be ignored.

In this piece, Karen shares some of her unfolding transformative journey from a limited, narrowly defined, isolated existence to a more authentic way of being in this world with an open and vulnerable heart.

Karen envisions a more deeply connected and compassionate world where individuals feel genuinely seen and can give voice to their personal stories.

If you are interested in learning more about Karen's story, you can find her at https://karenemifujii.substack.com.

Chapter 5

Rewriting Our Mother/ Daughter Stories with Love

By Tara Fries

One day last summer, I sat across from my beautifully dressed eighty-six-year-old Mother at a local diner for lunch after yet another long estrangement. We were discussing eyelashes or lack of them, and I said, "You always wore those false eyelashes." She looked directly across the table at me and said, "I always wore those eyelashes because I didn't like putting mascara on my lashes and having it smear under my eyes," "Aunt Linda had trouble with her eyes because of all the mascara she used." Ouch, my under-eye mascara always smudges!

Can we rewrite our personal Mother/ Daughter stories with our hearts? Can we meet one another in a new, joy-filled space, even if the "I love you, I hate you" still pops up? Yes, I believe we can. It's possible to rewrite the story, to alchemize it, even the difficult ones, when we choose to forgive from a place of no expectation; or not expecting that someone will ever "get it" or understand what they did. We must forgive ourselves also for our creation of it. It is then that we can fully move forward. That takes a lot of growth and letting go. When we heal ourselves, understand ourselves, and love ourselves, we can love another unconditionally with admiration and respect for who they are and who they have been for us in our story. We can appreciate their journey, too, and look at them with gratitude, compassion, and love as we hold that for ourselves.

It has been a long journey back to a healed place for me and my mother. My own healing journey has been intense and prolonged. The Beatles song, "The Long and Winding Road," always comes to my mind. The wounding presented itself as malaise and a soft depression, even though I appeared to be happy in my life. I am a smiley person outwardly, maybe on the positive side. However, my own dissatisfaction with my shadow eventually led me to healing and to enlightenment. To know one's own self well is the key to self-acceptance and self-love. If we focus on all the gifts our mother gave us, like life itself, we find the best things about ourselves. And in our own healing, we are able to expand these gifts and recognize our own worth- that we are truly a gift ourselves.

When I say healing, I am referring to the healing of ancestral patterns in families that are reenacted from one generation to the next. By becoming aware of the patterns, we can heal ourselves and heal our lineages. Our children won't have to undergo the healing we faced because we did it for them. I fell into it because of always seeking the truth and looking to better my circumstances. Everyone around you heals when you take on your own healing.

In the grand scheme of things, I spent more years not speaking to my mother than speaking to her. We mirrored each other. She abandoned me; I abandoned myself. In a bigger context, we were toxic feminines. It was easier to shut each other out than to discuss our rage calmly, to keep the love in mind, and to find peace. But that was our consciousness at that time. The "she said, she said" played out in drama for years. Every time a big issue came along, it was shut out time, time and time again. And there was that spiritual battleground between us- The Roman Catholic Church versus the New Age Spirituality. "Did you go to church today? Yes, I went to my own church- the Tara within." I would reply impatiently.

In 2015, seven years after my father's shocking passing, my mother went on a spiritual quest to Peru. You see, we are both seekers, prayer warriors, highly intuitive, and somewhat psychic. That's more mirroring. She has often told me that she heard a voice say "Corazon, Corazon" on her climb up the mystical mountain of Machu Picchu. She knew she had had a profound heart healing on that mountain.

The same year, I finally committed to my spiritual journey by joining an online spiritual membership and mentorship group. I had been seeing many synchronistic signs and was curious to learn more about them, and it all turned out to be a window to my spiritual gifts. And actually, the very beginning of an intense quest for spiritual knowledge. Which then led me to the healing modalities. I had many sessions with healers and began a daily meditation practice. As I committed to exploring my spirituality and divinity and I began to heal, my mother experienced her healing, which initiated a reunion between us.

We had been in separation from the time before my father fell ill in 2008. I was never informed he was critical or invited to his bedside alongside my siblings, even though he was dying. "Your Mother is not herself; forgive her," my grandmother cried to me. I was guided to my father's bedside the day they took him off life support. As my mother has always said, "God is in control." My brother and sister were livid, assuming Mother had told me to come. This was not the case. I was guided by spirit to show up, guided as never before. But I still found it hard to believe that a child would not be included in a final goodbye. In fact, I was truly excluded. Shut out. I was wounded and traumatized by that for many years to come, even though unseen realms so beautifully guided me to complete with my father. A hospice nurse said to me, "What could you have possibly done to deserve that?" My mother could not stand up for me to my sister's hate and jealousy, and in a recent epiphany, I realized that my parents had always given in to my sister throughout my childhood. To them, her word was the truth. Or maybe they knew I was the stronger one, so they appeased her, allowed her to manipulate, and protected her at my expense. She got an apartment in New York City as a single girl stomping ground after college, and she got a car during high school. I believe this seeded a pattern in me of not being a priority and going from dependence on my parents to dependence on a partner—a partner who would manipulate me and who I would over-give to earn their love.

Move the clock forward another 15 years, and I've got three darling grandchildren who adore me. My Mother would like to be part of my wonderfully joyful world again. We had been separated again. But now, my daughters are adults, and I do not want to let her in. How do I stand before them? My increasing awareness of the importance of compassion, empathy, and forgiveness on the spiritual journey will not allow me to go down the separation road again, so I remain committed to remembering the love with my mother. In spite of my daughter's opinions, I continue to be in daily contact with my mother, as she was a huge support to me when I chose to leave my relationship of 39 years. Then, financial issues with my ex got choppy, and I had to stand up for him. When I felt our settlement was unfair to him. My daughters still resent her for this. I view it as a gift that she even helped me get out of my prison.

A few days before last Christmas, I was having an angel reading. "Tara, your mother came to me yesterday and might come through today to tell me a few things." But she never came into the session, choosing to not come forward. She is angry because my daughters do not want her included on Christmas Eve. How can I turn against them when they have been my world when she wasn't? Why do things have to still be this way? Oh, because more is coming up for healing. So she disappears for about six months in lieu of a Christmas Day meeting. I am furious this time. We are going deeper with the healing of this family trauma. I am advised by someone I trust that my soul will be splintered if I don't forgive her and reconcile with her. Ahhhh. After I took a course on forgiveness, my mother called me and dropped flowers off for me on my birthday in June.

Our second meet-up after that is the one in the diner, where she remains somewhat cold to me. The eyelash jab and all. Did I mention that she is wearing a pin on her jacket's lapel? It's a dagger. I ask her what it is. She says it is the sword of truth of the Holy Spirit." I chuckle.

Can we come together in joy and forgiveness? I am thinking of going to the city for a class. One of my teachers will be in town at a metaphysical bookstore. My Mother invited me into the city to visit with her one-day last summer at her apartment in Manhattan. It coincides, so I plan to go. When I told her about the class that evening, she asked if she could come with me and then ride home with me to her house. How will I let my mother into my protected spiritual world? She might embarrass me as she often does with her big, no-boundary personality. But I realize it is a divinely guided healing for both of us and a wonderful opening and opportunity for me to share my spirituality, so I say yes to her and obnoxiously ask her to please "keep your mouth shut."

Ha ha, like that might work. "Mom, we will be hearing about multidimensional beings, star seeds, etc... Are you sure you would be interested?" The daily churchgoer says yes, she does have a guide she calls Cosmo. "Tara, I am interested.' She takes over the meeting. She asks the speaker, who is a psychic medium, "Why don't my children get along?" I get nervous. But he offers her this beautiful wisdom that is without blame, that includes, "Sometimes it's better to have space with one another. We don't have to be together. This is perfect advice without making anyone wrong. In love, we are blameless. We each got to ask the psychic a question. I do not ask a question but allow him to bring something forth for me instead. My Father's spirit is channeled through in front of my mother. The medium says my father says I have his strength, and I should use it to barrel through to get into my desired career as a life coach, working on it while keeping my job in the meantime. Now, every once in a while, my mother asks me, "How is it going, Tara?"

It all served a bigger purpose. She was able to hear and understand that I have bigger plans and aspirations for my life. I gained her energetic support. My desires were all exposed due to grace and divine assistance with her fears and my own fear of a possible financial downfall.

I have learned boundaries; she has learned boundaries. We love, laugh, and even discuss touchy topics, but it is because of our deep respect for each other that we can stay in our hearts. Maybe also because I do write down an intention if I am to meet with her, "Let my mother and I be happy with our time together today" or "Angels, please let my Mother know that I love her." I do catch her listening to me about my view of spirituality now, and she exclaimed recently, "I must be doing something right," when I received several surprising and generous gifts of love and thanks from clients this Christmas season. But the true gift is that we are able to be with one another now. The true gift is that we are living from our hearts.

About Tara Fries

Tara Fries is a life-loving, inspirational & enlightened healer/teacher and Certified Life Coach. Tara is a Divine Wisdom Oracle and Channel. She is a native of Long Island, New York, and is passionate about her connection to the divine, the expansion of human potential (including her own), and her family! We will heal the world with love, first by learning to truly love ourselves.

Chapter 6

The Script Rewritten

By Caroline A. Janssens

Beginnings

Mum comes from a family of six in Belgium. Her hard-working parents did all they could to provide for their children within their limited means. Being a younger daughter, Mum was designated less important in status and was often made to feel less intelligent and generally not enough. Being resourceful, Mum rose above these challenges by learning to be independent, copy the behaviors of others with higher status, and become an expert in her specific areas of interest.

After leaving home, Mum impressively earned her nursing degree and lived independently, which was most unusual in those days. Mum was driven by a desire to feel important and contribute in ways that mattered. As a registered nurse, her patients and supervisor loved her work and often praised her.

Key Turning Points

At 34 years old, Mum married Dad, 15 years her senior. They were a beautiful and close couple that others greatly admired. At the same time, their personality contrasts were quite evident. Mum was temperamental, while Dad was always calm and centered. There rarely would be a clash, and if they resolved their different viewpoints with deep love, understanding, and forgiveness. Mum and Dad's loving marriage lasted 25 years until Dad suddenly passed.

A prior critical turning point in our family was when Mum bore a second child a year after I was born. My little sister lived only a few hours before passing. Her birth and death took quite a toll on Mum. She required life-saving surgery to live and "made it through the needle's eye," as they say.

After that, when meeting other parents with young kids, Mum would often tear up. She continued to grieve her second child for years. During Mum's recovery, I was sent to live with my grandparents for half a year and saw Mum occasionally. I constantly begged her to hold me, but her health did not allow it. It left me with an imprint of feeling left behind and alone, which may have led to my tendency of wanting control and perfectionism.

Importantly, dealing with this tragic loss drove Mum to see me as a toddler throughout my life to adulthood. To this day, she considers me her 'baby'.

Growing Up and Expectations

Mum is a wonderful example of someone going the extra mile to give all she can to those she loves. She was a dedicated caregiver to her mother and father in their dependent years until their passings. In addition, she, together with Dad, looked after an elderly aunt living in a retirement home.

She takes her care of the household seriously and went out of her way to serve both Dad and me, but she still does. Though early in her career, Mum stayed home as soon as she became pregnant with me. She funneled her love of nursing work into caring for me and the house and always being ready when Dad and I returned home. Over time, she evolved into being the primary decision-maker at home.

For this hard work, Mum expected a level of participation, such as tidying the house and keeping my room clean. Mum's overbearing nature somehow added to the frustration. Her protective nature makes her consistently caution me to be careful, such as insisting I wear a scarf even in temperate weather.

Keeping a tidy home became a burden to me when I wanted to selfishly focus on my interests. This led to many arguments that, at times, ended up being blown out of proportion. Not only did I ignore the messes, but I took her efforts for granted rather than appreciating the care we received in our well-run home (which I expertly messed up again in no time).

Tumultuous Mother-Daughter Relationship

It may be no surprise that Mum and I share a stubborn streak and occasional temper. As a child, I clashed with Mum's household routines. She also always "saw the glass as half full," whereas I am a "full glass" person. My efforts to change these attitudes were frustrating and futile.

Even more contentious was our (unconscious) competition for Dad's attention. I received quite a lot of his attention. Though Mum loved me as her daughter, her inherent insecurity led to her feeling she held second place and I was a threat. This likely triggered her childhood traumas. Dad and I both loved to learn. We were always sharing what we were reading and studying. Our philosophizing on topics occupied much of our days and evenings. Mum told others I inherited my father's brain but secretly felt left out.

Mum and my differences triggered verbal arguments over many minor things, which I easily shirked off. With frequency, she would say:

"You never pay attention to anything in this house."

"You're so careless."

"You lack the interest in keeping a nice home."

I still hear my hear Mum's voice in my head on many days!

As I got older, I made the decision to pursue a career abroad. Deep down, I was ready to move away from Mum's influence, criticism, and disapproval. When I met my own partner, who became my husband, Mum was still not open to my differing points of view. In my view, she was unwilling to look at things through my eyes, which continued the wedge between us. I couldn't stop reacting to her treating me as her child frozen in time.

Healing and New Beginnings

It has taken several years for me to see Mum as a wonderfully kind woman and affectionate lover to my dad. I have gained many insights into her grief from unexpectedly losing her best friend and soulmate.

Also, as a woman in a long-term relationship with my soulmate, my own perspective on my relationship with Mum became different. I came to desire a harmonious, even delightful, mother-daughter bond which I have deep-down always been longing for. As Mum's actions pushed my emotional buttons and her critical words cut deep, I became aware of my own childlike reactions and emotional behaviors. To do the healing, I have made many internal adjustments to become more loving, calm, and understanding.

From participating in various in-depth personal development programs, I got to understand that it is up to me to own my responsibility in our relationship. I started to understand that I was the problem and the solution. I wished to heal our relationship. To do so, I took time to journal about my thoughts, emotions, and actions daily, which were more intense before and after my visits to Mum. I take time to feel gratitude for Mum's loving care and all that I receive from her. This practicing of gratitude I did daily and still do.

Also, I envisioned a harmonious mother-daughter relationship and how it would look and feel. I imagined Mum sitting at the kitchen table and giving her a daily morning hug. I saw us laugh together (Mum's laughter has always been so contagious), and we had enjoyable conversations filled with wisdom and joy. By holding this vision, I can now celebrate this exciting new relationship as it has come to fruition.

Another outcome from our relationship is that similar to Mum, I have chosen a career direction to help other adults understand and transform their beliefs, emotions, habits, and traumas. My knowledge and purpose are based on the extensive internal work I have done to understand myself, my Mum, and our mother-daughter dynamic and reach a place of peace and harmony.

Not only do I enjoy this transformed and evolved relationship, but I invited Mum to move in with me and my husband! I am ready to give Mum all the love, care, and attention she wants and deserves. The story has wonderfully come full circle.

About Caroline A. Janssens

The author started off in the corporate world and built a successful international career. She worked in senior positions in several international organizations, which brought her living in and exposure to all corners of the world: USA, Europe, the Middle East, and Asia.

Significant health conditions started to appear and literally brought her naked and to her knees. Through experiencing the adversities, her greatest learning and growth appeared. Caroline not only transformed back into health, but she also created a completely new life for herself. She runs a successful coaching practice, is a successful investor, and owns several properties, including her residence, which is a chateau in France where she lives with her husband and her horses, cats, and dogs.

Continuing to make this world a better place, Caroline is now contributing her share by helping individuals reconnect with their abundance and passion, one conscious mind at a time.

Chapter 7

Journey Home To Love

By Patricia L. Lai

I've always seen Mum as my hero. From my earliest days, she was the quiet strength in my life, a gentle soul whose kindness radiated from within. She never raised her voice; she didn't need to. There was a calmness about her that spoke louder than any words. When others complained about strict parents, I felt grateful. Mum wasn't like that—she was sweet, loving, and understanding. Whenever a spiritual teacher asked us to think of someone who made us feel loved, I would always think of Mum. She was my first thought, always.

Mum was a hardworking woman. She had to raise five children, which was no small task. And she didn't just raise us; she nurtured us to be our best selves. People would marvel at how well-behaved we were, and we did well in school, always bringing home good grades. We were a small, adorable family of four girls and one boy, and people often admired us. Mum was the center of it all: our rock and guide.

Mum was like a busy bee, always in motion. She'd wake up before dawn—long before the sun kissed the horizon—to prepare breakfast for us. It was never just a piece of toast or a quick bowl of cereal; Mum cooked hot meals every morning. Her food was a comfort, a warm embrace that started our day right. After breakfast, she would pack our lunches, and with five of us to feed, you can imagine how busy she was! Then came the cleaning—she washed all the clothes by hand, hung them out to dry, and ironed them to perfection. Back then, there was no washing machine, so everything was done manually. Despite all this, Mum found time to sew and was incredibly creative, always coming up with clever ways to fix or make things around the house.

I still remember my needlework classes at the all-girls elementary school. Each year, we had a different sewing project, and in our final year, we had to make an apron with our names embroidered on it. We used those aprons in our Domestic Science cooking classes when we moved on to Junior High. Thanks to Mum's meticulous ironing, my apron always looked perfectly starched, with every pleat neatly in place. I would proudly tell my teacher, "My mum did the ironing," and I thought the world of her. Oh, Mum, how I adored you!

Mum's wisdom always amazed me. She seemed to know exactly what to do, even in the most unexpected situations. I remember the time a snake appeared at the front of our house. With Dad often away for work, it was just Mum and us kids. When the snake slithered back into its hole, Mum quickly boiled a pot of water and poured it in, and we never saw that snake again. Bravo, Mum!

But life had not been kind to Mum. She was given up for adoption as an infant and raised by an elderly woman who needed help around the house. Even as a little girl, Mum had to work hard. There was no electricity, no running water. At just about five or six years old, she was sent to fetch water from the well, and twice, she fell in. Imagine the fear she must have felt! It makes me wonder if those experiences shaped her strong intuition and deep spiritual understanding.

Grandma, her adoptive mother, was strict, and Mum received little affection. She was often punished, made to kneel for things Grandma disapproved of, and had no freedom to speak up. It breaks my heart to think of what she went through, especially during World War II, the period of Japanese occupation of Malaya, which disrupted her education and changed the course of her life.

Eventually, Mum met Dad and started a new chapter. They had four girls first and then a boy. My childhood was filled with happy memories of playing with my brother and sisters and the neighborhood kids. But I also had my share of health issues—nosebleeds in the sun during PE and an enlarged lymph node on my neck. Mum would take me to Chinese herbalists, and I drank all sorts of bitter soups made from roots, herbs, and even dried seahorses. The symptoms would disappear for a while, only to come back later.

Upon growing up, I moved away from home and built a new life with my husband in America. In 2013, I faced new health complications—itching all over, rapid weight loss, and digestive issues that baffled the doctors. I felt lost and decided to return to Malaysia to see my family and celebrate my 50th birthday, hoping that being home would help me heal. Dad had passed away a few years earlier, and I was eager to see everyone, especially Mum.

But the warm welcome I had imagined wasn't there when I arrived. Mum seemed distant and uninterested. She didn't even want the gifts I had brought her. I was heartbroken and confused. Where was the loving mother I remembered? I knew she had aged and faced physical challenges, but I hadn't expected such coldness. I felt like I had lost her, and the pain was almost unbearable. I had been informed beforehand that due to her growing older, personality changes had occurred as part of her aging process and that she was not the same as she was before. And yet, I was totally unprepared for it.

After returning to the United States, I sought solace in spirituality, hoping to find healing for my body and soul. During a guided meditation, I received a vision of my birth. I sensed Mum's disappointment that I wasn't the boy she had hoped for. I was the fourth girl, and she was tired. She wanted a boy, and I had unknowingly disappointed her. It was a painful realization, but it began to make sense of the distance between us. I had often assumed that Mum was just happily giving birth to all of us and did not have the slightest clue that things were not as simple as I had thought. It suddenly came to light that my birth had not been well received. I was not the child my parents were hoping for.

I sought the help of healers who sensed that childhood traumas had contributed to my health issues. Each healer saw patterns pointing back to my early years. I realized there were deep-seated feelings of unworthiness within me, feelings I hadn't been aware of. As a newborn, I had tapped into the vibration of rejection because it felt like I was an unwanted child. Unfortunately, I could not release the vibration, and it was cemented in my heart as a truth that ultimately brought years of suffering. I had believed I was unlovable and not good enough for Mum and Dad. I then began a journey of forgiveness—of Mum, of Dad, and of myself. Through prayer and spiritual guidance, I slowly began the healing process.

I returned to Malaysia twice more to see Mum before she passed away. Though I was better prepared, I still struggled with the pain of seeing her unwell and the uncertainty of whether she would accept me. I knew, deep down, that she loved me despite what happened at my birth, but the emotional wounds were still raw. I did my best to make the most of those visits, honoring her with compassion and understanding the difficult life she had led.

After Mum's passing, I continued with my spiritual journey, seeking healing for my own pain. In time, through a healer, I understood that Mum had unknowingly passed on her emotions to me. I discovered that I had absorbed not just my traumas but also Mum's—her feelings of despair and disappointment when I was born a girl became embedded in my body through breast milk when she was breastfeeding me. The milk that carried her dismay, anger, and sadness became my nutrition, which laid the energies that formed my physical foundation as a human being. I did not feel safe nor secure.

Mum's emotions may not have been mine, but the charge from these emotions were very real. These emotions, when coupled with my own, created a burden too heavy to bear, leading to chronic health conditions that had plagued me for years. It wasn't enough to clear just my energies; I needed to release Mum's energies, too. Her feelings of hopelessness and her struggles had left an imprint on me, affecting my health. But through deep healing and spiritual work, I found acceptance, peace, and understanding. I came to see our relationship as a sacred agreement—a journey we both needed to take to help each other heal and grow. When I was able to see with clarity and understood the agreement, I let go of judgment and could comprehend from a higher perspective through the lens of love and compassion.

Through prayer, meditation, and deep divine guidance, I gradually released the emotions trapped within me. One day, in a moment of deep prayer, I asked God to show me how to forgive fully. Right after I prayed, with my eyes still closed, I was transported through a trance-like state to look inside a container in front of me. As I stood there staring inside, I let out a gasp as I felt a wave of love wash over me, and I realized that Mum had always loved me in her own way. I saw all the ways she had shown her love, all the sacrifices she had made. I saw how my parents loved me through their loving actions and conversations. And in that moment, all the pain melted away, and I found peace. I forgave Mum for the hurt I felt and myself for the resentment I had carried. My prayer was heard, and my eyes, heart, and mind were opened to see the truth, and I was free.

Now, I feel Mum's presence in the simplest of things. Pennies appear on my path, little signs that remind me of her love. Mum started leaving me pennies ever since she made her transition to spirit form. When pennies pop out of nowhere, I intuitively know they are from her. I cherish these moments, knowing she is watching over me, guiding me still. I am grateful for the journey we shared and all the love and lessons she gave me.

I honor Mum for all she was and all she continues to be in my life. I feel much love and admiration for Mum. She is my hero, guide, and everlasting love source. I love you always, Mum.

Through this journey, I also learned that healing is not just about curing the body but also about healing the heart and soul. It's about forgiving the past, embracing the present, and trusting in the love that remains. I was haunted by the past but was unaware of it. I couldn't find joy. When light was shed on the past, I understood. I was able to heal, forgive, and release.

The journey taught me to see beyond the surface and look deeper for the real truth. Through reflection, I realized I was holding on to the fear of rejection as a result of perceived rejection experienced from the time of birth. I was trapped in so much fear and insecurity and yearned to be accepted by everyone. The irony of it is the more I was afraid of rejection, the more I experienced it. This realization helped me release the fear, return to love, and create from love and truth. Life can be experienced quite differently when seen through the lens of love and hope. This includes loving myself with kindness and affection. I make peace with the truth of who I am. I honor, respect, and embrace myself with compassion for everything that I am and do, knowing I am worthy and good enough just as I am.

No matter how tragic the past may have seemed, I recognize I have the gift of voice to speak and share the truth of love. This is my journey home to love, to discover my true self and innocence before the corruption of mind took over. It is about finding my inner light and liberating myself from old beliefs which I had unknowingly taken on as truths since the beginning of my life. I settled the internal conflict within, and I made peace. I accept and love myself.

For decades, I did not see myself for who I truly am. I was looking through the frightened eyes of a little child. I now see with clarity through the eyes of love and grace. I am filled with gratitude, and I get to live life anew, knowing I have the power within to make conscious choices. I chose to walk away from the cage that I had unknowingly trapped myself in with a false sense of security. Instead, I choose to return to love, practice, and live love every day.

My husband and I recently took a trip home to my birth country. I had done the healing work, and the universe responded in kind by blessing us with a most wondrous and unforgettable magical journey. The trip was fully packed without ever a dull moment, and not only did I enjoy my bonding time with my siblings and other family members, but the trip was also productive, enriching, and exciting, with lots of exploration, which included exotic food and fun adventures. Plenty of resources were made available for me to accomplish the things I wanted to do, and I was richly blessed materially and financially as well. Most of all, I am grateful for all the love and attention, kindness and support, and generosity showered upon us by family and friends.

This memorable journey has solidified my faith that I am a worthy being and that my light makes a difference. I see and love myself as the girl I was born to be, recognizing and owning that I am whole and complete and that I am enough just as I am.

About Patricia L. Lai

Patricia L. Lai worked as a corporate professional in the hospitality and financial industries for over twenty years before taking a leap of faith and walking the spiritual path. She obtained her Master Law of Attraction Coach and Quantum Energy Master Certification from the Quantum Success Coaching Academy, founded by Christy Whitman.

Having lived in two different continents, Patricia sees the world from a broader perspective as she embraces the richness of cultural diversity of both Eastern and Western cultures.

Patricia enjoys writing about her life experiences to inspire and entertain through her stories. She takes her readers on her transformative journey of self-discovery, where she finds her true self and her voice and falls in love with the self whom she never knew before.

Chapter 8

The spiraling pattern of healing

By Heidi Zin

I had an early love for seashells and a rather large collection. I love tracing the spiraling patterns, backward and forwards, marking time. I am a keen observer of nature and how everything is connected.

My early conditioning was shaped by a tradition passed down through the female line. I was taught to be attractive, agreeable, and courteous. To be seen yet not heard. To wipe the smile off my face, lest I be viewed as mischievous. I was to be obedient and not go against his word, "my way or the highway." I was discontent with the law of the land, yet I dared not make waves. I was in an ancestral societal training to give my power away. It's not that I was unloved, not at all; I was provided for, but the conditioning of my behavior was deep and thorough. I felt something was inherently wrong with me. Thinking to myself, I had a voice and creative ideas, but I was not often encouraged to use them. Quite the opposite. I was instructed time and again to leave it for someone else.

I was the middle of three children. I remember having feelings from an early age of not belonging, being on the outside with thoughts like "if I was hurt or if I was famous, then they would love me. (this did not prove to work out to my advantage). I remember as a child watching my mother, who was beautiful and trim, always holding in her tummy, checking herself repeatedly in front of the mirror. She would compare herself to other ladies in the neighborhood. I was perplexed by this. I did not, at a young age, understand that my mother felt insecure about herself. She doubted herself and her voice. She expressed to me that she wanted an education. She compared herself to other women in her circle who had a higher education. She didn't feel her voice was adequate, that she had something worthwhile to offer, even though she had helped put my dad through school. She pitted herself against other successful females at the time, in the 60's. She was made to feel small and to be non-threatening in order to protect and support him. It felt like mom was tormented to have attention. I watched as she appeared to feel pushed aside, with her ideas being valued as less than his. I wanted this for her as a positive role model for myself. When I expressed my feelings or ideas of inequality, I was told I was too sensitive, and that's just the way it is. I got used to it, and it was all in my own mind. I gradually learned to mistrust myself. To be quiet, to retreat, and to doubt my own innate guidance system. This would turn out to be deadly for me. The subordination I felt was shaming. My feminine spirit was sacrificed "and" banished, and I was afraid of myself, so I began to hide. I felt most comfortable out of my body and invisible, yet it was not comfortable at all. I was learning to abandon myself so as not to be abandoned by others.

Looking back, I don't remember my grandmother's voice. She passed away when I was fifteen. I do remember her beautiful flower gardens that she spent hours tending. Shucking peas, husking corn in the fall months, and canning food for the winter. She made yummy lemon meringue pie, but I don't remember the sound of her voice. She was a wonderful musician, so they said. She was trained to be pretty, polite, and pleasing. She wore gloves to church and a hat with a veil. It hung before her face from her eyebrows to just below her chin. Covering her mouth as if to hide gently behind. To be seen and not heard. I saw this hat to be peculiar and absurd, fashioned for the time.

I don't remember my mother holding me much. I grew up feeling a cool breeze of resentment bubbling underneath as she peered behind her cigarette smoke, Virginia slims menthol. I was fascinated by the way she could French inhale and move the smoke around in circles out through her mouth, in through her nose. I grew up believing my mother resented me. I

67

resented her in return. I spent a lot of time alone, creating, reading, or out in nature. I loved the natural world; I felt freedom from my constraints. I was adventurous. I wanted out. There were very few words of encouragement, more like words of correcting disapproval. I yearned for her to tell me stories of her life, her dreams, and who she was. She would flatly reply, "I don't remember." I learned to keep things to myself, to not share my stories, and to avoid eyes of disapproval at the dinner table.

My father was a good man, and he showed love, which was the only way he knew how. I was provided for and protected, but I wanted more depth. I yearned for closeness. I felt outside the established system I was raised in. Things in the home felt somehow superficial, and I was not connecting. Part of my conditional training was learning to serve a man. I bucked; I wanted my own life. If I wanted something and asked, instructions would come, such as "leave it for somebody else." You don't need to make too much money; your husband will take care of you. This confused me. I wanted something more. My dad would call my sister and me derogatory names based on our body images. I was embarrassed and found my name offensive, Skinny Bottoms. My younger sister was Minnesota Fats. He thought it cute. I did not have a voice to correct him or to say that it hurt. My mother never came forth to correct him in front of me. She remained quiet. I hated her for this. I wanted her to come to my defense. I wanted her to see my anguish, to identify with me and the shame I felt smoldering within. I wanted her to see my pain. I went further into myself, or rather out of myself.

I rebelled as a teenager. I had to hold up a sword to protect something rigidly instead of just being authentic. I did not know at the time that I was abandoning myself. I just had to get away from the stifling pain, but it followed me. I left home early on. I wanted a college education. I moved to California and got myself into junior college to prove that I could go to school. I did well in school. I was always an overachiever, especially when it came to creativity. I had talent, and I was going to make my mark and prove that I was lovable and that my voice was valid. I wanted to be heard, to be considered, and not pushed aside as being inferior or cute. I ended up getting a college degree in Fine Arts from a reputable College. Graduating top in my class, and yet it still didn't seem to be enough. I was still caught up in giving my power away. I remember thinking I would never have a relationship like

68

she had. I wanted my mother to have more of a backbone to be able to speak out against injustices. My mother wanted to have a job and to be able to earn money. She wanted more than being a housewife; she was talented at interior decorating. She would help friends, but she gave it away for free, and she was not allowed to have a job to earn money. She received an allowance. I was not going to be stuck in her situation. She didn't have any authority over herself; she couldn't; she had to be pretty, pleasing, and polite. She was the social entertainment organizer, and she excelled at it.

I was the first female in my family of origin to receive a degree in higher education. After I graduated, I went on to work in a museum. I helped curate a show where I met my future husband. I thought I had found something new, someone that supported me. We were going to be artists together. Unbeknownst to me, at the age of 27 I walked into and embraced the same familiar pattern of neglect and belittlement that I experienced growing up. On our wedding night, I felt in my soul that something was off. I quickly found out that I was in the same type of relationship where my voice was not considered equally, if at all, even though the players looked different. I was labeled dramatic and dispensable. I did not feel valued nor taken seriously by my husband; he came first, and I served his career. There were also less-than-desirable nicknames that he found funny at my expense. This pattern had already been laid down, and unbeknownst to me, it was embedded in my DNA. I knew myself to be a kind, compassionate person, ready to jump in at a moment to help somebody, yet he labeled me otherwise. I spent a lot of energy trying to get him to understand, "No, you don't see me. That's not who I am". My voice of defensive yearning fell on deaf ears as I was labeled "not fun." It became an impossible situation for me, one I didn't understand yet but was oh so familiar. The wounds I had sustained growing up, I would not be able to fully unravel, nor would I understand the patterning for some time. After a couple of years of marriage, I had the feeling that I didn't belong. I was suffocating and buried under the pressure. Something was terribly wrong. I flew home and asked my parents if they could help me get a divorce. My mother scolded, "You made your bed; now go sleep in it." Shocked at the inconsideration, I flew back to California the very next morning. After all, it was not something she could have ever done herself, even if she had wanted to. That was the conditioning. To stay and make it work. There was just one problem: In my marriage, I was invisible, and my voice didn't count. It was hard to navigate. I was suffering a lack of support and becoming invisible even to myself. Resentment and friction built up, and like my mother's sentence to me, I was labeled too sensitive. I did end up getting a divorce. I felt freedom for a while, but then this old pattern of no voice and internalizing what other people thought and said about me would hold me hostage. It would be a pattern that would persist for many years.

I would return every so often to the family of my upbringing. I desired healing and closeness. I loved her and them. I was diligent in my returns. Around my mother, I somehow always felt outside, being compared to not good enough. It was in me, and I didn't get it.

As a visual artist, I struggled to show my work. Speaking my ideas around it and being visible and being heard was somehow against the grain and I didn't quite understand why or how to fix it. It was an internal struggle within myself. I would chastise myself, questioning, where was my voice? My confidence? And my internal power source? When I did speak, I would often blurt out my words too fast or too loud, or I would hold my thoughts to myself, knowing that I knew yet could not speak forth, holding onto my words. I experienced an internal feeling of self-loathing and of being shut down. I felt uncomfortable in my own skin. I sought out counseling, thinking something was off with me. I had dreams, I had desires, and I had talent as a visual artist, but it was as if I had a straight jacket on, conditioned to give away.

I began to look at myself with a bit more depth. I drew the internal patterns, and the emotional feelings associated with them. I became interested in shamanism. I started to understand the ancestral patterns being passed down with a bit more clarity. I was able to see the karmic line and began to loosen the grip it had on me. I had always felt sorry for my mother, wishing that she could have pursued her dream. She had a good life, but she was missing an inner fulfillment. I had more opportunities than she, yet our closeness would remain just out of reach.

Years later, my mother was to come down with the deadly pancreatic cancer, and I had the opportunity to spend the last couple of months of her life with her. Upon arriving, I felt like I didn't belong somehow in the family, with my brother saying, "You don't belong here. You've never been here", and me thinking, "This is my mother. I love her, of course I deserve to be here". My mother and my sister were very close. I struggled with my feelings of being the outsider, yet I was going to take my rightful place.

When my mother was on her deathbed, a few things happened that would change my perception of the situation. The first time she saw me when I returned, she screamed out, "I'm going to hell." Oh dear, I thought. I reassured her that she wasn't going to hell; she was going to go be with the angels. On another occasion, as we were shifting her body, she spoke out, "I have a right to my own body, don't I"? In this moment, a realization flew across my mind, "this woman never even felt she had a right to her own body." Not only was it her voice, her livelihood, but her own body too that she didn't feel she had a right to. I thought about this long and hard in relation to my own experiences. I had deep compassion for her, for us. Another thing she said to me was, "I never gave you any credit, did I"? This was the only apology or understanding I was to ever receive from my mom. I realized in that moment the pain she must have endured, quietly seething under her skin. I realized at that moment that perhaps she didn't resent me as I had thought all along but resented instead her time, era on this planet, and the social conditioning of women that she had to endure. She expressed a need to die before my dad because she had a real fear of not being able to take care of herself. I reassured her at that moment that I would always take care of her. She could move in with me. She looked at me and said, "You would do that for me," like she doubted it because our relationship had always had friction, the friction of wanting more, of knowing you could do more than you are allowed to do. We had been stuck firmly in patterns passed to us. After her departure, Dad questioned, "Why did I prevent her from working"? He then turned to me, "go do your art and live your passion.

I knew there was a better way; something in me continued my search. I went to kirtans, I worked with nature Spirits, and I went to Lakota fire ceremonies. I did art therapy for release. Kali Ma became my goddess, the great destroyer and rebuilder. Through shamanic journeying and, eventually, plant medicine, I started to see how I had denied my own feelings to make it okay for others. I began to look at and explore some of these deeply ingrained cultural patterns that held me back. I was going to find my voice.

I was going to express what was deeply inside of me that needed to be expressed. I believed I had more to contribute to the culture than I had been allowed. I saw how I had to sabotage myself to fit in and be acceptable. To fend off men who would offer an opportunity to my art career if I slept with them. I had a right to my own body, didn't I? After all, these were not real opportunities for me. I began to question why I was always doubting myself, second-guessing myself, and asking myself what was going on. What was real? I created artwork around it, trying to excavate the ancestral pattern that I imagined as a string going back and forth through us, connecting us. I recognized a pattern that was holding me in place, and I felt somehow that it was my job to untie from these repeating ancestral patterns. I went on an inner search. Through shamanic journeying, I met and spoke with ancestors, I met power animals, and I worked through situations, redreaming the dream. One journey, I heard loudly, don't be the bunnies, be the bear. I started to gain Inner Strength and understanding of myself. I learned I did not have to internalize what other people said or thought about me. I was beginning to embody myself and my own beliefs around my own capacities and talents. I slowly started to gain use of my voice. I was no longer willing to live in a superficial relationship with myself or anyone else who didn't feed me. I was becoming self-aware, and I liked myself as I embodied my own body and my own being; I had presence.

I started to become aware that my body couldn't lie. I felt what I felt, and it was correct for me. The mind, on the other hand, could tell stories. During one plant ceremony I participated in, I questioned, to spirit, "How can I love myself even more"? I was dancing with sound-canceling headphones; it felt so good to move my body. My eyes were shut, so I didn't see anyone observing me, and it felt good. I started to feel a bubbling sensation coming from my fingertips, moving up my arms through my fascia while I was dancing, like 7Up under my skin. I laid down in a fetal position to stretch; I was in the child pose. All of a sudden, I was in a vision of long ago. I was a teeny tiny baby, and my father had my arms somehow in his hands. Standing over me, I was in a scene of conditioning. I was being conditioned on how to be, how to act, how to behave. I was being controlled, and the pattern was stored in the fascia under my skin. Off in the corner, I could see my mother standing, a little image of herself. I looked at the scene. I looked at it closely and felt the feelings. I saw her. In that moment, I realized my mother had gone under more severe conditioning of repression than even I. At that moment, my perception changed. I had deep, deep compassion for my mother. I loved her and all she gave. I understood the lineage of ancestral patterning. I could clearly see the pattern of no voice, little movement, and the message "leave it for somebody else" I had heard growing up. A message I had absorbed that had dictated and controlled my behaviors. I watched this pattern for quite some time. I felt the compassion run through me until I had found complete forgiveness. I realized in this moment that this forgiveness was for me, for all the struggles I had gone through. I understood; I was fully seeing the pattern of struggle to find self. I felt I belonged right here, right where I was, right in this body, with this voice, with this mind, with this understanding. I was an integral part of this ancestral pattern, and I was here to help unravel it. How many times had my mother been quieted, her mother and their mothers? How far back did it go, the suppression of will?

In the days that followed, I noticed that the pattern started to shift. Opportunities appeared, and family members reappeared. I started to notice that some of the same circumstances that had happened to me had reverberated through the ancestral line, yet we had never been able to speak about it. The grip was loosening. By not forgiving an ancestor or myself, I realized it was keeping me from the freedom to seek, speak, and share fully where I felt comfortable. I had freedom, and I was finding my voice in a world that was superficial. I wanted my mother and my grandmother to know. I wanted it to reverberate down the ancestral line. I think somehow, they're heralding me from the other side. My search for my voice, my belonging, and my right to be here will help my descendants, and I believe it will help my ancestors as well. The story we tell has energetics that affect everything all around us. It's a vibration. I had been on a lifetime journey of changing the dynamics of my ancestral vibration through the female line. I had broken the mold, and the conditioning of my upbringing slowly began to shift, altering the future of history. I experienced a shift in my consciousness that would reverberate all down the line and into future generations. Like the spiraling pattern of the seashells, the trauma also held a pattern that spiraled through our generations. It begins to unravel, and there is a sense of release and freedom. I declared I BELONG. In my declaration, I included my dear mommy and grandmother. I am not afraid of myself any longer. I am releasing myself from the victim perceptions that have defined my life.

The story of the feminine to be sacrificed ends now. She is not dangerous; I am not dangerous.

I learned that by being in touch with my own power, I can be gentle and respectful and smile in the face of someone's attempts to play power games. I learned to embody my own power. I am the power and authority of Heidi. This is my reality—power within, not power over.

One of the last things my mother said to me was, "If you see a penny on the ground, think of me." I have a large jar of them.

About Heidi Zin

Inner Medicine Woman Artist

From a young age my art has been a constant rhythm in my life. I have always felt an intrinsic pull towards creative expression. Color, shapes, lines, patterns, and textures became a form of understanding and communication with the world around me. My works are inspired by the natural beauty of the earth, human emotions, and the interplay between light and Shadow. I am deeply influenced by the element of water, Shamanism, and a search for inner meaning. These interests form a personal sanctuary of love, fun, Mastery, and a connection with others. I studied art and received a BFA in sculpture and drawing from CCA and the San Francisco Art Institute. I also hold a certificate in the expressive healing Arts. I have received several awards, one being the California Discovery Award issued by Henry Hopkins for my early environmental series. I spent decades teaching art, knowing and sharing that creativity is a valued foundation. I receive direct transmissions from Spirit for my creations. I have always had a keen interest in healing my own inner world, and I was open to what needed to be revealed. I learned to dive into patterns of entrapment, generational wounding as well as societal conditioning. I have explored the transformative power of creativity, and with this understanding, I evolved and claimed the title of inner Medicine Woman artist. Through my art I invite others to witness the beauty of transformation and to embrace the healing potential within themselves.

www.zinart.com

Chapter 9

Legacy of a Life Lived in Love

By Alli Nathan

Motherhood. Magnificent. Mystical. Marvelous. Like Mother Earth, our mother's ground and guide us all their lives, and as daughters, we offer gratitude to glorious and graceful women who are our mothers. Endless number of words paint pictures of mothers and motherhood—some loving others hateful.

I imagine my awareness of my mother's feelings when she discovers my presence in her - the wonder she felt as she sensed me growing inside her - the beginnings of brain and spine, head, ears, eyes, mouth, arms, and legs. She hears the fetal heart pulsing (110 times a minute)—the heart exactly the size of the baby's fist.

Ah! Baby's first kick and punch. What a delight! Baby's fingers, toes, and nails are taking shape. The baby is responding to pain, light, and sound. With heart, brain, lungs, and diverse internal systems in place, the mother senses the baby is ready and impatient to come into the world.

I want to be with this wonderful woman who has been nurturing me for the past nine months and for the last three months amidst her grief in losing her son—my brother—who was a year and a half old.

I feel my mother's physical pain and emotional strength. She wants the excruciating and all-encompassing pain to go away and everything to be over, and then it is over. She feels emptiness inside her and is anxious about the life that has come into the world. She waits breathlessly to hear me cry. She is overwhelmed by everything in and around her. She sees her mother cut the umbilical cord and take me away for my first bath.

Then, I am in her arms, swaddled in the blanket that she made with her son's baby clothes. I hear the familiar sound of her bangles and smile at the safety it implies. Multifarious bangles were placed on her hands a few months ago as she was welcomed back into her family with a celebration called "valai kappu" (bangle protection), a tradition that creates the bond between mother and child through the sweet sound of bangles.

My mother softly caresses my head and hair, ears, cheeks, nose, lips, and chin. She smiles at the black dot on my forehead at the third eye anointed with a paste made from blackened rice to ward off evil eyes of ill-wishers.

She looks into my eyes with tears in her own eyes as she also feels the tragedy of her son's untimely death. Then I see her radiant smile, meant for me and only for me. My life begins when I see her smile, and I look into the duality in her eyes— sadness and happiness.

She hugs me tight with a wish, desire, and determination to protect and nurture me in her own image. She was my mother—my AMMA, the beautiful word for "mother" in Tamil, my language.

Her wish was my privilege.

***

My mother was the magician who made her sorrow and depression invisible to us - her four daughters, who were born within ten years of her devastating loss. She had the support of my father, who was also suffering from the untimely passing of his son, and sometimes talked about what could have been. He wanted his dreams for his son to manifest through his daughters.

Our parents were two suffering souls unable to connect with and comfort each other. But their shared vision for our futures allowed them to support each other in their endeavors. In a culture dominated by patriarchy, my parents were applauded by friends for their zeal to nurture and inspire their daughters to achieve their dreams.

My mother was the driving force. She let the memories of her son reside in the deepest corner of her heart, mind, spirit, and soul as she showered us with unconditional, limitless love and devoted her life to our happiness and success.

She had the steadfast backing of my father, who ardently supported her ambitions for us. After all he married her for what he perceived as prescient yet prudent values intrinsic to her and her family. My father was an unseen presence who embraced and endorsed my mother's independence and passion in nurturing us to be avant-garde in our own way.

My mother's legacy begins with her desire and determination to be our confidante and mentor. In her eyes, daughters were as valuable as sons. She empowered and encouraged us to be strong and independent professionals—experts in our own field—and explorers to roam the world as she had when she moved to England to be with our father when I was a year old.

We are in enduring awe of our mother's amazing achievement in a culture that is more misogynist than Western societies. Daughters are considered a curse on the family, an onerous burden to be foisted off to another family with appropriate "dowry."

Dowry is a tradition that requires brides to bring money, goods, or estates to marry into the bridegroom's family. A custom to provide monetary security and status for the bride in the new family, it has degenerated into a reprehensible practice of exploitation and abuse of women, especially when the dowry is considered insufficient by the husband's family.

She made waves in this orthodox society, going against the ethos of the culture by empowering and enabling us and granting us permission and privilege to follow our dreams. It is as if she sensed that her daughters were unique, valuable vanguards, just as she was.

She created an atmosphere of freedom without the frustration that afflicts many intelligent women in India. She created opportunities for us to walk our own paths, even if it meant a hidden sadness and sorrow in her as we departed our hometown and eventually our country.

She celebrated our achievements as professionals and to the surprise of the skeptical society, she guided us to find our life partners and rejoiced in our weddings. She is our inspiration as we steer our daughters to achieve their aspirations and dreams.

***

Maya Angelou said that mothers will look after us and anybody who needs to be looked after in any way possible. She brings her whole self to us because she is our mother.

My mother was a divine soul whose destiny was to be present for anyone who needed to be cared for—family and friends. She was the sage and savior that everyone relied on. Anytime, anywhere, she was a paragon of grace and virtue.

Our mother always seemed to know when we were in crisis, even if we were far apart. A letter in her beautiful handwriting would arrive just in time to give us comfort, love, and light. Her letters made everything look less fearful and more beautiful.

Her magic has passed through generations as my nieces experience the same love and magic in their mothers. Here's what my sister's daughter said of her mother: "The characteristic that always fascinated me was wherever we went, everyone knew my mom because she was the queen bee. It made me want to be like that and be a leader but also always kind to everyone and serve my community."

Poet Robert Browning: "All love begins and ends with motherhood." As I reflect on a typical day in my mother's life, I am touched by her effortless energy and doubtless devotion to us.

For many years, the famous four "Nathan Sisters" were all at the same school, and our mother would be at school with hot lunches for us. This ritual started when my youngest sister was in kindergarten to avert tears of anxiety in the three-year-old.

Again, my sister's daughter: "My best memories are the care and love my mom always shows—when we were small, she left for work so early but always made us lunch and wrote us a note in our lunchbox, and then always showed up at three o'clock sharp so certain people (her brother—added for clarity) wouldn't cry. Also, I remember lots of books, reading together, and doing silly art projects."

We also expected our mother to be at home in the evening to greet us with drinks and tiffin when we got back from school—she always was.

After lunch and before we got home in the evening, it was our mother's own time. She spent it doing what she liked the most—reading literary works: historical fiction, murder mysteries (Georgette Heyer, Agatha Christie, Perry Mason, anyone?), historical and current non-fiction, news magazines, and newspapers, both in Tamil and English. We inherited her love of reading, which we passed onto the next generation - our daughters, now reading with their children.

***

Our mother was an English Literature major and having lived in England and Australia early in her married life, she realized the value of English as the language of the future. We were educated in private schools with English as the language of instruction.

She was our singular champion, who fought for what we needed and desired - at school and in society. She was confident in our talents and fiercely argued in favor of her oldest, who was refused admission at school, and her youngest, who was harassed by teachers for being left-handed.

Her tenacity in a conservative culture was admirable, and her unlimited love for her daughters allowed her to champion our non-traditional ambitions and shenanigans.

I did not want to get married at sixteen, and my youngest sister wanted to wear jeans—both were a no-no in India at the time. I wanted to travel the world in a job that fit my global mindset. Two of my sisters wanted to train as anesthesiologists and pediatric cardiac surgeons in the UK and USA. Our mother guided and cheered us all the way to achieve our dreams. Many criticized her conviction and confidence. Isn't that what happens when a society encounters trailblazers who are trendsetters?

I was an academic and now an aspiring creative writer. My sisters in the medical field have both contributed to fine-tuning anesthetic procedures and innovating research designs to measure outcomes in cardiac surgeries. My youngest sister leveraged her biomedical research skills to design and offer niche products in colorful Indian fabrics.

***

Every moment of Mother's life was filled with love for us. She never said no to any of our dreams but was determined to guide us on our path to being independent, successful professionals. Our success is a tribute to our mother's wishes and dreams. We are here only because she wanted us to be. A mother's love is omnipresent, and a mother's legacy is omnipotent. Our mother is evidence of these undeniable facts of life.

Mothers are the essence of our being, the nucleus of our existence, the pillars of our support, and the cornerstone of our lives. The mother-daughter bond is everlasting. But what happens to the daughters when the mother suddenly, unexpectedly dies, leaving the daughters to fend for themselves?

My parents were on their dream trip around the world, and they were planning to visit us in the UK and USA. Their first stop was with my sisters in England. To ensure that my mother's heart was strong enough to handle long and strenuous trips, she was admitted to the ICU for overnight observation of her weak heart.

But her heart chose to attack with a ferocity that filled her lungs with blood, making it impossible to breathe. She died holding the hands of my father and sister, whispering to my dad, "Take care of our daughters."

Those were her last words. Even in death, she was thinking of us. Thus, she died in England, where she spent the early years of her married life. Was that a coincidence or a conundrum?

She was fifty-seven.

***

Let me skip all the crying and sobbing except to delineate my dad's despair. My mother had been his love and life during the thirty-five years of their marriage. We could see anguish and distress in his eyes as he sat in the living room with tears, with a look so vacant. He died at ninety-seven, having lived with the tragedy of having lost two people he loved the most—his son and his wife.

We felt helpless and hopeless. Seeing my mother later in the funeral home was surreal. She looked as if she was taking a nap before going to the British Council Library. There was an inkling of her beautiful smile. Was she really dead?

Yes, she was. Yet, she was not. She will not be with us in the physical domain to be a part of our lives. But when we were in different countries— far away from her—she seemed to have been with us, like a protective shadow and a mystical angel.

Will she be there for us? Or do we have to navigate this 21st-century chaotic world by ourselves? Why did she leave us? Is it because she felt confident we will live and thrive in this chaotic world without her? Is it because her angelic presence was needed somewhere else?

Sometimes, we resent our mother for leaving us because we miss her poignant presence and yearn for her prescient power in mentoring us. We have learned to live with gratitude and admiration for all that she was and still is in our lives. We believe that is her wish for us.

At her funeral, we shared memories with laughter and tears in abundance. We realized how her beauty, warmth, grace, and love for us were reflected in all things large and small.

My sister remembered the five weeks she spent at the British Council Library copying by hand all five hundred pages of an out-of-print medical text. My sister treasures that manuscript. The other students used their incomplete class notes. My mother wanted her near-genius daughter to have unfettered access to the book so that she could continue to be the top-ranking graduate in medical school.

A vivid memory of my youngest sister is the radiant smile and smiling eyes of my mother as she embraced my sister every time she came back home from college on an overnight train. Mother welcomed daughter every time, without fail, at six o'clock in the morning. How can one ever forget the timeless love reflected in her smile and eyes?

Now, as our nieces and daughters leave home and our hearts break, we understand the immense sacrifice our mother made by hiding her broken heart with her beautiful smile and warm embrace when we left her to pursue our lives.

Despite wanting us to be with her, she was willing to let us go to achieve our dreams. Through us, she lived her dream of being an English teacher and writer. Behind all our success stories is the story of her success.

***

This may be a cliché, but Amma never left us in spirit. We often feel her loving presence around us. My sister says that when she is feeding, bathing, or playing with her three-month-old grandson, she senses our mother's enigmatic smiling presence.

A generational inheritance! A special kind of pure maternal love, invisible to the world, integral to Indian culture!

My grandmother was the epitome of motherly love in nurturing me for the first ten years of my life. I remember spending an hour every evening with her as she immersed herself in prayers, the words still echoing in my ears. My mother cared for her granddaughters on and off till her death. My sisters now carry on this tradition by caring for their grandchildren and embracing the dreams of their daughters.

Motherhood has no generational boundaries—it's a never-ending cycle of love. Our mother was the "be-all and end-all" of our lives. Our millennial daughters value this heritage, and we are their guiding light. But I am sometimes surprised by the GEN Z generation of daughters overwhelmed by our warmth and affection. A generational shift, perhaps?

***

Infinite number of bilateral, reciprocal relationships exist in the world - in the political arena among nation-states - no love lost; in the animal kingdom - amazing friendships; and in the human realm - a multitude of connections.

In the multiplex of human relationships, none is as authentic, effortless, and harmonious, yet none as complex, conflicted, and convoluted as that between a mother and daughter. It is fraught with physical, emotional, and psychological conundrums.

The connection between a mother and a daughter created when they look at and feel each other at birth is embedded in their souls and spirits forever. It is a bond that is enigmatic and esoteric, beyond our knowledge to understand and our power to destroy.

The manifestation of mother-daughter symbiosis as loving or hating is driven by the sometimes tranquil and sometimes turbulent elements in the cultural, societal, and familial environs around us.

Despite my accolades about mothers, I acknowledge that not all of them are perfect. While evolution hardwired all children to need their mothers, it did not hardwire all mothers to care for their children.

As the children grow into adulthood, only about half of them are blessed with loving intimacy with their mothers, while the other half suffer estrangement from a malicious hatred that defines the relationship. With current solutions being futile clichés, will epigenetics offer an answer?

We were blessed and privileged to have an amazing, caring, joyful, and loving mother-daughter relationship. We live today with incredible memories to share about our mother's legacy of a life lived in love and light. Hard as it may be to believe, our mother was the manifestation of pure love, untainted by hate. She was the melody of music and the delight of a dance.

We aspire to live in our mother's image, inheriting her unconditional love and unwavering care. She taught us to live with grace and generosity, with love, light, laughter, and much more. Beautiful memories carved out of our mother's incredible life journey are forever ingrained in our hearts. We treasure this and say BRAVO! to all mothers of this world.

Thank You, AMMA.

About Alli Nathan

Ms. Alli Nathan, PhD lives in Montreal, Canada. She is exploring a new career in creative writing, writes short and long essays, and is working on a memoir dealing with defeating depression. She is passionate about teaching and writing as tools for empowering and encouraging others. She is a graduate of the University of Madras, India, and Queen's University, Canada. In her previous career as an academic, she interacted with GenX and Millennial students, instilling in them a love for sciences and arts - finance and history. She has lived and worked in the EU and the USA, a reflection of her global mindset and fulfilling the dreams of her parents and grandparents - a trailblazer and a trendsetter. She finds her essence in nature, yoga, and meditation, which augments her writing. She loves to research for leisure and read for pleasure.

Chapter 10

My Two Mothers

By Beatrice Andrade

I grew up thinking I was lucky to have the most loving mother in the world. The ironic thing is- my "mother" was my grandmother and not my biological mother. I always felt safe, seen, and cherished by her. I can still feel the warmth of her hugs any time I was sick or how she would make a warm cup of chocolate milk for me to help me feel better.

My grandmother was the matriarch. She was strict, always running the household to her liking... spic and span. She had seven children and never missed a beat. I remember her small flower garden in the front of the house with the lovely smell of roses as you would step out onto the front patio on a rainy day. The scent always made you feel light and warm, as if you were truly safe and at home. She also had a small vegetable garden in the backyard. I always felt happy as we bonded while we would gather vegetables to cook for that night's dinner. She gave me the example of how to be a nurturing caretaker. She even had a small store inside our home where she would sell homemade snacks to the kids in the neighborhood. These kids would not only come for the snacks but also for advice. She always seemed to have time and energy for anyone in need and was so giving. I always admired her for that. She showed me unconditional love that I did not see anywhere else in my environment at that time.

My mother, on the other hand, was different from her. She was raised to fit the traditional mold of being single and was kept by my grandparents until she was ready to leave the home. She went to a religious school up into her early 20s. Between the two strict environments, she did not have much experience with life outside of the places where she went. Due to the lack of guidance from my grandparents or interacting with other people in social settings, she was very naive.

I experienced what felt like abandonment from my mother. Throughout my life, she constantly made choices in people and circumstances over me. I felt she could never take responsibility for what she had in front of her before she would take the leap into something else that would only create more difficulty in her life. I always perceived her as weak, irresponsible, meek, and broken. Later in her life, she would continue with a pattern of choosing men who would be abusive, neglectful, and deceitful to her. Unfortunately, I would be the observer of that. She was not able to make beneficial and healthy choices due to the experiences she had about being controlled as a young woman.

I found it disgusting the way she had been treated by the men in her life. Many times, I saw how she was abused both verbally and physically. This created a substantial amount of trauma by seeing these detrimental actions take place right before my eyes. To see a woman being shamed and treated so horribly would later taint my own life. These instances were so severe that I still believe, to this day, that my brother's birth was induced by physical abuse she had endured the day before she went into labor. I can still remember the times she would cry so deeply I could hear the pain in her voice- yet she had no voice. Nothing she said mattered. Not even in her own home.

When an opportunity arose for her to change her ways, she again made the choice to repeat the cycle of her past. Because of this, it was very hard for me to get close to her. I had no respect for anything she said or did and, more importantly, no trust. I decided that everything I would do in my life would be the total opposite of what she did…especially in the role of mother.

The experience that I had between these two women, I later realized, formed me into what I became as an adult. The influence they had over me went well beyond what I considered my own choices. My sheer will to either be or not be like them would not be enough.

During my younger years, I would always remind myself of how I NEVER wanted to be like my mother. I would constantly think of how to do things differently. I decided early on while being persuaded by my grandmother to finish my education. I truly believed this would be the way out. This would be the solution to having a better life and experience than that which my mother had.

The first years of my life were spent with my grandmother, during which I was happy most of the time. Even though we didn't have much, I still remember how much love she poured into me and her home. This was the true substance of what created such a strong bond between us. I noticed this "special" treatment was given to me, more so than others, but I didn't understand "why" at the time. At the age of 7, my grandmother's health started deteriorating, so it was not possible for me to continue living with her and my grandfather. This separation was difficult for me. They had been my safe haven until now. One day, out of the blue, one of my aunts came to pick me up. She was so mean to me for crying hysterically for what was about to happen. The act of being pulled from the only home I had ever known was no less than tragic for me. I felt like my insides were being torn out and like I was losing all hope. I didn't understand how this much pain could be possible. I cried for hours during the trip back to live with my mother. This was a turning point for me, and the rest of my childhood would be very tumultuous.

Living with my mother was not pleasant for me. She and I never had a true connection, and I didn't feel like I could trust her. Even though I did seek her love and attention, I always felt she had so many other dramas and distractions that kept her from being there for me. At this point in her life, she had remarried. Her husband was abusive and unstable. We felt as if we were walking on pins and needles any time we were around him. This created a hypervigilance for both of us. As the years passed, there was a lot of moving to different homes, different types of abuse, both to me and around me, along with the chilling expectation of where or how we would end up. With these experiences, it created a state of constant fear. I learned early on how to protect myself and developed hard survival instincts. This was far from the more peaceful reality I had experienced earlier in my life.

All this abuse would mold my perceptions and beliefs about being a woman, relationships, men, and life. As a child, I didn't know this. I was simply absorbing all the information around me, which was slowly creating a "mold" of what LIFE IS and what was considered "normal."

I knew and felt deep inside that there was something wrong with this picture. My family was very religious, so I would question everything. I didn't understand how God would allow such horrible things to happen to people. I became quite rebellious about continuing the family tradition of being a religious individual. I thought, "If these are the results, they are living from being devoted to God, how could life possibly get better?".

I would always seek out ways to "escape" my reality. This curiosity and determination to not repeat the living circumstances I was experiencing helped me to dig myself out of that reality. I was determined to finish my education and get a degree. I made plans in my mind to begin traveling. I wanted to become a different version of a woman that was not typical of my ancestral traditions. I knew there had to be more. I made a promise to myself that this would not happen to me. If I became a mother one day, these patterns would stop with me.

Before I knew it, I was a young adult ready to graduate. I was so proud of myself for making it this far, regardless of all I had endured until this point of my life. I had a deep desire to continue on my path to college, but there was a change of plans. During my senior year in high school, I became pregnant. This would change my life forever.

This was not easy for me to accept, and so I bounced around with the idea of having an abortion. This was not part of the plan, yet something very deep inside of me would not let me do it. I cried and cried over this new life growing inside my body and thought, "I will do my best to give him or her the life and opportunities I did not have." I made an effort to become close with my husband and married him. This, I thought, was the solution to breaking the family pattern of not having a father, as my mother had done with me. I was proud of myself for recognizing this. I felt eager and happy to do this, knowing that by this action, I was also influencing someone else- my unborn child.

My mother was present at my wedding ceremony. She was in my room while I was getting ready, and she told me, "You don't have to marry him." I was shocked! This made me so angry! How could she say this to me? Had she no idea of how I grew up? All the disappointments I had endured and felt because of an act such as this? I told her that I would not do as she did. That it had been hard enough for me being fatherless and that I would give my child the chance of having theirs. As before, she simply remained quiet with no words of encouragement. This deepened the grief and discord I had against her.

Finally, the day my son was born was here, and it was one of the happiest days of my life. This tiny miracle changed me inside. I felt myself come alive and full of hope. This child would give me the courage to move forward and regain the optimism I had lost about life. The first time he was put in my arms, I thought to myself, "So this is what unconditional love feels like." I was in awe and wonder and so happy that I had made the choice to have him. In many ways, he gave me strength and I felt that now my life had purpose.

As the years passed, I grew in many ways as a mother, wife, and professionally. I felt and believed I was making great strides. I thought I was "defeating" the unhealthy life and family patterns that I had grown up with. I was very protective of my son, family, and home, and I did everything I could to be the perfect mother and wife. I worked hard as well to prove that I was growing and becoming something that none of my relatives had accomplished before.

I had created a new family through marrying my husband. I thought my life was going well…until one day. It was my father-in-law's birthday. My mother-in-law always seemed to have some sort of resentment towards him, and I never knew why. I would always ask myself why she was so mean to him. In my own way of feeling sorry for him, I decided to graciously have a dinner party for him and even bake his favorite cake. As the party came to an end and people left, I remember my mother-in-law arguing with my husband about allowing him to stay the night. He had been drinking, so I told her that it would be ok if he stayed and that we would make sure he got home the next day. She seemed reluctant but agreed. Little did I know this would turn my life upside down.

I went to my bedroom to sleep while my husband stayed in the living room talking to my father-in-law. After I fell asleep, I was awakened by some very strong fondling. I was under the impression it was my husband, as I had my back to him and told him to stop. He continued. Finally, the touching became so intense I turned around to tell him no, and to my demise, it was not my husband, but my father-in-law. Next thing I knew, the light turned on, and my husband and son were standing next to my bedroom door. My husband looked at me and asked what was going on. I started crying hysterically! All I saw in that moment was my son's eyes. I could not believe that THIS was happening to me in my own home! My husband asked me immediately to take my son and leave our bedroom. I was terrified at the thought of what could possibly happen next.

What was this? Why me? I could not understand how I had been working so hard to make sure that this type of incident or abuse never happened to me again. I thought I was doing everything "right" to prevent these patterns from reappearing in my life!

My husband and I stayed together after this, yet we never discussed it. This incident unraveled a whole other realm of secrets, which would create more chaos within the family. He also spiraled into drug addiction, not being able to deal with this new reality. I could not believe this was happening! I was so dazed and confused, and it all felt surreal.

How did I deal with all my pain, anger, and suffering? I forged ahead. Why? Because this is what my grandmother did during a crisis. She was the only woman I looked up to, so I, too, would mimic her behavior. I was the matriarch now, and so I paid no mind to my pain, needs, and health. I did everything I could to continue living our life the way it was before and neglected my own pain. I had to make sure "everything" stayed as "normal" as possible and keep my son safe.

My marriage was never the same after this. We fought and moved a lot, and yet I still thought it was all normal. I started having health issues and panic attacks. This was my body warning me, yet I did not know how to "listen" to it.

I didn't have the support I needed to help me understand and unravel all the unhealthy conditions I was living in. This was the first time in my life that I felt I needed my mother. I reached out to her for help, and she said she couldn't because she had too much going on and that she wasn't in good health. Again, as during my childhood, I felt this as abandonment, though it was now years later. I felt so defeated. I felt like I had no one. Yet, the mantra inside my head was "Stay Strong."

A couple of years went by, and I learned my grandmother was entering the last days of her life. She had so many health issues at this point. I went to visit her, and she pleaded with me to forgive my mother. I told her I couldn't and that I wouldn't due to the lack of love and care from her. I told her my only mother was her and that she was the only one I had ever needed. When I left, I asked myself, "Why would she ask me to do that?". I didn't quite understand. She passed away soon after, and my heart was broken. She was such a tremendous loss for me; I couldn't bear it. It would add to the layers of pain and sadness I was already holding, and it would take me years to heal from this grief.

The loss of my grandmother and the stress from my wreck of a marriage made me even more ill. I found myself having debilitating migraines and issues with my body while still sticking to appearances and pretending I was ok. The constant pain and grief finally made me realize I was living a life that no longer "fit" me. Soon after, I asked my husband for a divorce. I left the job that I had had for many years, which had supported me through all the difficulties. In some way this had been the only pillar in my life at that time.

After leaving these behind and feeling somewhat better, I unwittingly followed in my mother's pattern. I quickly got into another relationship and became pregnant. Once again, I recognized the same pattern, yet this time it was different. I would have an abortion. This would be, unbeknownst to me, another deep heartbreak that I would carry with me for many years.

At this point, I knew my life had to change, but this time starting within me. I decided to begin my healing journey to heal all the pain I was carrying inside of my body. A path of self-discovery and truly beginning to understand the fabric of my life. How everything that I had experienced until this point was no accident.

I started searching for a shamanic healer. I thought this would help me begin to understand what was ailing me from deep inside. After our first visit, I went home to take a shower. I screamed in pain for hours. I had never screamed this loud in my life, ever. The agony I felt coming through my body brought me to my knees. I was exhausted.

After a couple of days, I asked myself, "What was that?". How is it possible that I had all of this pain inside of me, yet I was unaware of it. Even though I was so uncomfortable after my session and going through this, I actually felt relief in my body afterward! This was something deep that had happened to me, and I decided I needed to know more.

I began studying spiritual sciences. I wanted to know what had happened to me that day and why. I quickly became fascinated by what I was discovering. I realized that there was so much more that I had no control over. I began studying energy, biology, ancestral patterns, and how they affected me.

Through several years of studying different types of religions, such as Buddhism, Hinduism, Kabbalah, and more, I began to understand the interconnectedness between mind, body, spirit, and the soul's evolution.

All of this, along with changing my lifestyle, led me to higher self-awareness. Understanding the experiences that had "happened to me" was simply a reflection of what I had inside of me. My body slowly began to heal. My health became better, and I started to naturally become happier. This healing also brought me to a space of not only forgiving myself but others who were part of the pain from the past.

After over a decade of healing myself, I came across Medical Intuition. I learned that the work I had been doing all these years on myself could also be used to help others heal.

One day, a client approached me about writing a book. I said yes. A couple of days after doing so, I intuitively heard that I needed to get the TRUTH before I began writing this book. This TRUTH was to come from my mother. I was shocked and confused. I had not spoken to my mother in a long time, and in my own way, I had already forgiven her. I thought to myself, what else could there possibly be?

I followed my intuition and called her. I was shocked to hear that she had been waiting for me to call. For the first time in my life, she asked me to forgive her. This was something that I had hoped for so many years. I started to cry and felt areas in my body that I had not felt before. The wounds were so deep. I realized in this moment that the TRUTH that I needed to hear was about to present itself.

Shortly after, I visited my mother. It wasn't easy. I had a lifetime of bad history with her, yet I knew in my heart that this would perhaps help me heal in ways I didn't know existed. This is where a huge part of my story was revealed to me. She began to share with me her version of the TRUTH.

She started by telling me she knew very little about dating when she first laid eyes on my father. She was naive to the influence that my father would soon have on her. Many times, she would question his position as a single man and whether he was being truthful. Due to a deceptive conversation, she had with his father, she would believe him and end up eloping. This would turn out to be a huge mistake. The gravity of this action would be carried out for many years to come.

Her running away broke the bond and trust she had with my grandparents, even though they had been controlling and strict. She would discover that my father was, in fact, already married and that his clever deceitfulness was simply for him to have a new conquest. At some point, my mother had no choice but to return to the home that she had so furiously abandoned. Her quarrels with my grandmother increased tremendously, and the tension in the home intensified. She soon also discovered she was pregnant! What to do? My grandmother immediately told her she was to abort! During this time, due to societal rules, it was deemed a shame and inappropriate for a single woman to bear a child. My mother struggled so desperately and deeply with this possibility. Regardless of the external circumstances that were presented to her, she felt in her heart that she wanted to keep this baby.

As fate would have it, my mother would have this child- me. She became ill due to the pressure my grandmother was putting on her. At her first visit to the doctor, who was to perform the procedure, he told my grandmother there was no way she could abort. The illness that my mother had needed to clear up before the procedure could be done. My grandmother was full of disappointment and rage, yet silently, my mother was grateful. As the days passed, one of her brothers stepped in to help by asking my grandmother to reconsider. That perhaps the illness that had come over my mother was a sign that this abortion was not to take place. By some miracle, my grandmother listened, and her determination to have my mother abort subsided. This predetermined fate would change her life.

As she told me about her experiences and what she had gone through, not only with my father but with my grandmother, I was shocked and in tears. I could not understand how it was possible that my grandmother, the woman who showed me so much love, could BE the total opposite to my mother. It was almost as if she was talking about a different woman. I could also see in her eyes how the betrayal of my father had damaged her in ways that were evident even to this day.

I began to cry even more as now everything was starting to make sense. Why I had silently felt the way I had my whole life! Feeling like I didn't belong like I wasn't wanted. Always being moved around as a child and feeling like I was an orphan, even though I was not. How I had this pattern with men in my life that were so similar to what she had experienced with my own father. I started to connect the dots. She had answered so many of the questions I had my whole life about certain events during my childhood, her story with my father, and her behavior towards me. I realized I had it all wrong.

We spoke for several hours. This is the longest I had ever spoken to my mother. I sat and listened with an open heart. I was amazed at myself for having the strength and the courage to do so. By the end of our conversation, I was holding my mother's hands and holding a loving space for her so she, too, could release her tears of grief. The burdens that she had been keeping quiet and carrying inside her entire life. In forgiving my mother, this would heal the generational trauma.

I went home with my mind in shambles. I asked myself how could it be that I had also been carrying this grief and grudge against my mother all this time. All the time, energy, and space that had consumed me by all this. What I had believed all along was not even the real truth. How believing what I did had also created a false identity for myself!

Later that day, I went to the lake and watched the sunset to help me continue processing what had just happened. For the first time in my life, I felt true peace in my heart. I had made peace with my past. I called my mother at that moment and told her, "I forgive you." The very thing my grandmother asked me to do many years before. Perhaps my grandmother had asked this of me due to the guilt she felt for how she had treated her own daughter. This story had come full circle.

Throughout this journey, I have realized how much influence our ancestor's patterns and generational traumas have within us. I also said to myself that if I had known this before, I would have asked my grandmother about her TRUTH when she was alive. How much did her truth influence her life and my mother's?

As a result of my life experiences and my healing this brought up in me the desire to help others. Doing this work has also helped me heal and transform the relationship I have with my son today. To help him recognize and heal the generational traumas and patterns for himself and change the trajectory of our lineage.

By truly understanding our heritage, with this knowledge, we have the capacity to change and to heal not only what is inside ourselves and our bodies but also significantly impact our external world and our future. This is True Power. This is Living. This is Transformation.

About Beatrice Andrade

Beatrice Andrade is a gifted Quantum Healer, Seer, Certified Medical Intuitive, and Alchemist. She has performed hundreds of sessions, helping her clients heal traumas, physical conditions, and diseases. Through Quantum Healing, she is able to heal generational traumas, subconscious programming, and spiritual ailments. With years of studying multiple energetic healing modalities and becoming a Certified Medical Intuitive, she is a Master at utilizing her multiple Clair abilities to facilitate deep transformational healings. Through her own healing and transformation, she is a testament of her work. During her free time, she loves to spend time in nature, writing, traveling, and spending quality time with her family. She has founded Spiritual Healing 777 to help others heal and discover their innate power and wisdom.

www.spiritualhealing777.com

@beatriceandrade777

Chapter 11

A Legacy of Love: Breaking the Chain of Abuse

By Shelley Whizin and Sarah Schultz

Introduction

Shelley: I first want to acknowledge and thank my beautiful daughter, Sarah, for being my greatest teacher and healer on mothering.

Growing up, I believed that love and abuse were synonymous. I thought it was normal. My experience was hearing, "I love you," then hit, hit, hit or yell, yell, yell. Being the oldest girl of 5 kids, I thought it was my fault that triggered my mother's rage, that I couldn't do enough to make her happy.

When she would lose control, she would hit one of us with a belt and make us all watch. We would stand there crying and yelling, "NO, MOM, NO!"

You would think that would have stopped my brothers and sisters from getting each other into trouble, but it didn't. We were taught to cut each other off at the knees.

I learned to walk on eggshells to make sure I was as invisible as I could be. I believed that I didn't matter since I was the one responsible for everybody's everything. Being in a house with scary frenetic energy was tough, I'm not going to lie.

Seeing my beautiful daughter as a resourceful, loving, kind, funny as hell, giving, smart, exquisite mother, open to learning how to break the chains of her foremothers just thrills me to no end. I know that when I am gone from this earthly plane, she will continue with the tools that make her strong and continue to pass on her insights to her children and grandchildren.

Breaking a generational chain is one thing, but breaking the chain of abuse isn't just about stopping harmful behaviors—it's about replacing them with something better. For me, that meant love, understanding, and a commitment to growth. It requires looking at the pain you've experienced, understanding it, and making the conscious decision to create something different—not just for yourself but for the generations to come.

I knew I couldn't change the past, but I knew that I could change the future. And that future started with my daughter, Sarah. It's not the easiest thing in life, but so what? It's possible, and I feel blessed to be proof of that, as is my daughter.

If I died in the next moment, I would already feel successful that I was able to break that chain with my daughter, as she has empowered her daughters, Jordyn and Zoe, to be all they can be as strong, resilient, and loving young women.

Sarah: I was fortunate to grow up with a mother who broke the "mean mold" and treated everyone with respect. Unfortunately, I knew all too well how painful my mother's childhood was and, fortunately, how determined she was to change how she raised me and the example she would set.

Everywhere I went, everybody would comment on how amazing my mother was. Day in and day out, I was reminded of how nice and supportive she was. My mother made a conscious decision to treat others the way she had always wished that she was treated while growing up by both her mother and her siblings.

While my mother nearly always exuded the respect that everyone desired, my childhood was far from perfect. My parents divorced when I was four years old, and I had my own trauma throughout the process. My mother and I didn't always see eye-to-eye, as my guard was often up. Trust was and has always been a challenge for me, and it didn't matter that my mother was a gentle soul; I was always waiting for the shoe to drop. I believe that my vulnerabilities at such a young age are what helped me grow both emotionally and mentally.

As I got older and wiser, I realized what my mom gave me was the greatest gift of all: a safe space to be who I wanted to be while showering me with support. That is not to say that she approved of all my decisions, but regardless of what she felt, she always treated me with dignity and respect. My mother worked hard to make a change, which helped me prioritize how I would end up treating my children.

This was when I started to believe that the legacy of love that she had started would continue for generations to come. Between our experiences in life, good and bad, we worked together to replace a legacy of pain with one of love. And I wholeheartedly believe that when my children have their own children, this legacy will continue.

The Origin of the Chain

Shelley: My childhood wasn't easy. Our home was steeped in depression, and my mother, Ruth, carried the weight of the world on her shoulders. She was sad a LOT, which turned into anger and rage, and was sharp and unpredictable.

I became a little mother at 4 years old when my sister Judy arrived, then to my younger brother, Mark, 2 years later, and then again to my baby sister, Andrea, 3 1/2 years later. My older brother, Ron, 2 years older than me, was left on his own.

I was responsible for cooking and keeping the house clean, ensuring everything was in order, and even making my siblings' beds. If something wasn't done, it was me who got in trouble. They knew it, too, and would taunt me, leaving their beds unmade just to watch me squirm. We were taught to tear each other down, not build each other up. No one ever asked, "How was your day?" No one was really interested in each other.

We were all afraid of my mom, never knowing what was going to trigger her and who was going to be hit with a belt or be yelled at. The frenetic energy was everywhere: morning, noon, and night. We all walked on eggshells, including my dad.

I was so afraid of my mom that I even hid the fact I got my period… for 3 days! And I didn't feel safe enough to run to her when I was upset about something. Instead of holding me in her arms, she would always say, "Is it necessary for you to cry?" I never got the comfort I needed and sought approval and validation from everywhere and everyone else, sometimes to my own detriment.

I know now that my mom was doing the best she could with her own sad story growing up. Her birth mom, Rose, died when she was born, and her dad, Jack, blamed her for her dying. He couldn't cope, nor even look at her, so he left for a year on the road selling hats while she was being raised by his mother.

When he came back, he married her mother's friend, Dora, who became the only grandmother I knew. They had four more children, who were treated differently than my mom, and my grandfather lived out his life as an angry man.

My mom told me that when she was eight years old, she found a letter in the attic saying she was "adopted," and at that time, it was shameful to be adopted, so she kept it a secret. My grandfather never told her the truth until she was 18 years old. No question about it: my mom had a painful childhood with her dad being angry all the time, hitting her with a belt (hmmm… I wonder how far back that goes?) Talk about a chain of abuse!

Her parents left South Bend, Indiana, for Los Angeles during my mom's senior year of high school. Can you imagine? That, in and of itself, is enough to hurt any 17-year-old girl. I think she was even in love with someone. Her feelings didn't matter to her parents, and so the generational chain of abuse and dismissal continued.

Then, she met my dad, Al, a Navy veteran, at a dance in Hollywood. They knew how to dance together. Have a healthy marriage? That was another story.

Of course, I realized later on in life that my mom didn't have the tools to cope with her own pain, and unfortunately, that pain spilled over on all of us. I was a pretty aware little girl, and I would beg her to treat her children with love, respect, and kindness, but she would always say, "You treat your children the way you want, and I will treat my children the way I want."

I remember one day mustering up the courage to tell her that all of her children were afraid of her. She made us stand in a circle, coming up to each one with her face in our faces, yelling, "ARE YOU AFRAID OF ME?" Everyone cried out, "NO, MOM, NO!" To this day, I don't ever remember why I ever got hit with a belt. What I did know was I wanted something different for my future children.

Looking back now, and after much therapy, coaching, and self-reflection, I understand that my mother wasn't a bad person—she was a deeply hurt one. She loved us but didn't know how to express it in a way that felt safe or nurturing. As a child, I couldn't see that, of course. I only knew I felt afraid, and I vowed that when I had children, they would never feel that way. They would grow up surrounded by love, not fear

Later on in life, I came to the conclusion that my mom was an "angel of pain," teaching us how NOT to be. I was determined to break the chain once and for all.

A New Beginning: Motherhood and Challenges

Shelley: When my daughter, Sarah, was born, I was filled with such tender love and determination. I wanted to give her the world, to create a life for her where she felt cherished and safe, comforted and loved. Unfortunately, my marriage to her dad wasn't what I hoped it would be. I often felt like that little girl again—afraid, powerless, and intimidated.

Leaving the marriage was the hardest decision I ever made, especially because I wasn't strong enough to stand up for myself at the time. What I did know was when Sarah was born, I would never hit her like my mom hit all of us. I knew it would be different. Ever since Sarah was a little girl, I did my best to instill values of love, kindness, openness, and trust with a lot of humor along the way.

Healing Through Connection

Sarah: Often, people connect via tragedy, and while my mother's and my experiences were vastly different, we both experienced failure before learning success. Her failures stemmed from a mother who was abusive and mean, while my failures stemmed from a broken home and a lack of trust. Together, we worked on creating a life where respect was the number one factor in all relationships, breaking the chain of abuse.

My grandma Ruth never treated me poorly the way she treated my mother. However, it was clear to me that the world's weight was on her shoulders, always causing her to complain and whine, especially when it came to my beloved grandfather, the apple of my eye. However, after a while, being around them started feeling icky, so I tried hard to mirror my mother's newfound outlook on life versus the negativity that constantly surrounded my grandmother.

In my teenage years, I started spending more time at my mother's house because I felt a sense of security and safety. I knew that no matter what I shared with her, I never had to fear her reaction. In fact, I never feared her, a total one-eighty from what she felt growing up. This was purposeful, this took work, this was intentional, and this was my mother. I knew with every bone in my body that my intentions would be similar when I had kids, and I never wanted my kids to be afraid of me. The value of love won in the end, and to this day, she is the one person I tell everything to, regardless of how I think she will react.

Both my mother and I have experienced life's challenges over the years, but one thing that has always connected us is how we treat others. In college, I knew I wanted to study people and how we communicate with one another. My interest in communications peaked after I realized how hard my mother worked to break the "mean mold," and I was determined to live the rest of my life trying to be like her. But, let's be honest, we all have our moments, and my "mean mold" may come out here and there, but my core intention is to treat others the way I (and my mother) have always wanted to be treated.

Breaking the Chain: Parenting My Own Children. A New Generation: Passing Down Positive Values

Sarah: Even though my mother was the prime example of how I wanted to treat my own children, I still had demons that felt like they would interfere with my core intentions of always presenting as kind and respectful. I'll leave out the details as to where these demons stemmed from for the sake of being kind, but they existed deep inside.

I was blessed with twins at the age of 26, and as a new mother with double the responsibility, I didn't know how to move forward. I faced my own insecurities and battled with postpartum depression, but despite it all, my mother and my husband were right beside me, treating me with the utmost respect. They didn't treat me as though something was wrong with me, but rather, how will we move forward and how will we get through this together? It was during these challenging first few months that I vowed never to be in that deep hole again because I had a support system that wanted me to thrive and stand by my side.

After four years, I was blessed with another daughter, and I knew this "closer" (in baseball terms) would be my last child. I (and my husband) had to break all "mean molds" that we had inherited and change the narrative. So, we did. I ensured that my relationship with all my kids, especially my daughters, was like the relationship with my mother. I wanted that closeness, trust, lack of fear, and support system that I had with my mother. So, I consciously applied the values that I learned from my mother, including love, respect, open communication, and joy, with my babies.

Nothing has changed over the last 19 years. We still have the same relationship where they know they can come to me about anything, and I will provide them with the space to be real, who they are, and support their needs. My number one goal is for my children to be happy, whether I particularly agree with their decisions or not. However, it is the way in which we communicate with each other that matters to me. I have certainly approached parenting differently after hearing how sad my mother was growing up. The cycle of abuse ended with my grandmother, and I am ever so appreciative of my mother for breaking the "mean mold" indefinitely.

Shared Values Across Generations

Shelley: Watching my daughter raise her children is one of the greatest joys of my life. She and her beautiful high school sweetheart husband, Mike, are the most devoted parents I have ever seen!

They are both raising them with so much love and intentionality, and it's beautiful to see. Her kids are growing up in a home filled with kindness, respect, and understanding. Sarah and Mike are great role models of what it takes to be friends first and have a healthy relationship as devoted parents. They're learning to express themselves, stand up for their beliefs, and navigate the world with compassion.

When I see them, I see the legacy Sarah and I have created together. It's not just about breaking the chain of abuse—it's about building something new in its place. It's about creating a world where love and respect are the norm, not the exception.

I beam with pride watching her become the mother I always wanted. She's done an outstanding job of showing her kids she loves them, respects them, and encourages them in whatever dreams they conjure up. She is the most devoted mother and genuinely cares about her children's well-being. It's just such an honor to witness her as a mom.

Sarah: It is extremely important to me to pass on specific values that I deem non-negotiable. Having empathy when going into any situation is imperative. I grew up wanting children and loved all the children around me. However, when it came down to it, and I had my own children, postpartum depression snuck up on me, and without the empathy from my mother and my husband, I could not have gotten through it all. Therefore, showing empathy to all, even without knowing their situation, is a must. Other non-negotiables for me are accountability, resilience, respect (manners), and kindness.

I truly believe that without failures in life, success wouldn't happen. However, the importance lies in HOW you deal with the failures and HOW you react/deal with them. My children know that there is nothing that I will not support them in as long as we deal with each situation with all the values

I mentioned above. My intention has always been to be open and transparent with my children the way my mother was/is with me.

I am so proud of my children for many reasons, but above all, they carry on the legacy of love and shared values. From the time my children could talk until this very day, I hear from others how my children's manners are exemplary. They say thank you and please for everything because they expect the same from others.

All three of my children go above and beyond to show kindness to others. When we lived abroad in Japan, we volunteered every Sunday at a homeless shelter. They would help prepare, serve, and clean up the food. Each Sunday that we volunteered, my children would come home with an appreciation for what we had, which in turn made them want to do more for others.

Lessons for Others

Shelley: Breaking generational chains is not easy. It takes work, determination, and time. But it's possible. If you're reading this and wondering if you can do it, let me tell you: you can. It starts with a decision—committing yourself and your children to do things differently. It doesn't mean you won't make mistakes; it means you'll learn from them and keep moving forward.

Sarah: Healing and change are part of a marathon; it takes work before, during, and after. It is not about being perfect (although I have OCD, and I love it when everything is perfect), but it is about showing up each day for one another with love and intention. It is about choosing to create a better future not just for yourself but for each other and the generations to come. Once you consciously decide to choose love over pride or anger and choose to forgive and move forward, the weight will be off your shoulders for good! And be kind to yourself because no one says this is easy. Anger tends to be easier to exude than kindness; I wonder why that is.

Conclusion: A Legacy of Love

Shelley: As I reflect on this journey, I'm filled with gratitude. Gratitude for my beautiful daughter, Sarah, who has taught me so much about love and resilience. Gratitude for my beautiful son-in-law, Mike, and my beautiful grandchildren, Jake, Jordyn, and Zoe, who are growing up in a world filled with hope. And gratitude for the chance to share our story, knowing that it might inspire others to break their own chains and create their own legacies… a generational healing that will go far into the future.

Sarah: Breaking the "mean mold" was hard but totally worth it. As I reflect on my life thus far, I am so grateful that my mother was able to do this early on in my life, which made it easier for me to recognize how I wanted to approach everything with my own children. As I look at my Jake, Jordyn, and Zoe and how they represent everything we have worked so hard to cultivate, it makes my heart so happy to know that they too will continue the shared values with their children and the generations to come.

I am proud that my daughters are strong individuals, growing up to be empowered women who have the courage to stand up for themselves and know they can be whatever they set out to be. My son has had a mentor in my husband and the way Mike treats me, his wife, and how he treats his daughters with the utmost respect. This is the kind of man my son is and will continue to be as he starts his own family one day. We are lucky and grateful and will continue to help people break their "mean mold" for generations to come. Lastly, I would not be who I am today if it weren't for the incredible mother that I have. We are different in so many ways, yet the same in our love for people (well, usually)!

About Sarah Schultz

Sarah has lived a very eventful life. She grew up in the San Fernando Valley with two sets of parents and three siblings. Sarah married her high school sweetheart, Mike, and they have three kids, Jake (19), Jordyn (19), and Zoe (15). Their lives have been nothing short of hectic, living in 15 different cities/states/countries in the last 20 years for Mike's professional baseball career. Once settling down in LA about 10 years ago, Sarah got her MBA and showed her kids that continuing education at any age was possible. The family currently lives in Valley Village with the twins off at college and Zoe in her freshman year of High School. Sarah is living out her dream as a dedicated mother, wife, and daughter to the best mom out there!

About Shelley Whizin

Shelley is a transformational life coach, death doula, and end-of-life trainer with over 30 years of experience teaching the human/spiritual dynamic. She helps clients reframe limiting beliefs, connect with core values, and navigate life's challenges with ease, grace, and joy.

A proud mother, Shelley broke the chain of generational abuse, creating a legacy of love for her daughter and grandchildren. Her own reinvention after cancer and divorce shaped her compassionate approach to helping others embrace their highest potential.

Shelley's background includes a degree in Jewish Studies, yoga teaching, a variety of coaching modalities, different cultural traditions, and extensive community service. Shelley empowers others to live fully, love deeply, and find meaning, even in life's most challenging transitions.

Chapter 12

Changing My Early Agreements with Life

By Christine Judal

A child's life is shaped by many influences, but the family we are born into shapes us most of all. Certainly, we arrive in the world as a truly unique individual, one who has never existed in humankind's entire history. As soon as we are able to walk and talk, we begin to demand our authenticity. Ask any parent of a toddler about how profoundly the child who wants something can fight in the moment that she is denied!

One of the most challenging jobs of a parent is to "domesticate" their child. For the first few years, all the rules are set and enforced by our parents and others who care for us. As we grow, we begin to make our own judgments about ourselves and our world. It's hard to overestimate the power of these early judgments and assumptions. They become agreements with life that powerfully impact and shape our experience long after we have forgotten the details of their creation. Our developing brain is designed to encode these judgments and agreements into "programs" that run in the background of our consciousness. This facilitates our development so that we don't have to keep learning the same things over and over.

Often, the most powerful background programs are the ones we unconsciously or semi-consciously create during times of fear and stress. These programs can stay with us for years or even lifetimes, determining how we perceive and interact with our world. As the saying goes, "What goes in early goes in deep."

Almost everyone has had the experience of having old, unhelpful programs from childhood that prevent us from living our lives in the most beneficial way. We are often not even aware of them because they are so integral to our worldview. But when life brings the agreement into focus, we no longer are bound to it. We can choose a new agreement, a new way to experience the world!

My story is about a certain dramatic experience in my childhood. This was a moment when I made powerful agreements with life that influenced how I related to the world—at least until I learned that I could choose a better way. Perhaps you may also remember an experience when you created a life-impacting agreement in your early life.

As is true for most families, mine held a powerful history of relationships and family dynamics. I was the sixth child born to parents who had been through many difficult times in their lives. My four oldest siblings were born into a family experiencing poverty during the Great Depression. Later, my father fought in WWII and was held in torturous conditions for nearly four years in a Nagasaki, Japan, prison camp where he intimately witnessed the atomic bomb from his prison camp just above the city. During the war, my mother struggled to feed and care for four young children. Thankfully, her German-born mother, nicknamed MemMem by our family, moved in to care for the children while my mother worked as a waitress.

After the war, my father was released from the prison camp. Unfortunately, my father and MemMem had never gotten along. It wasn't long before my father, in a drunken tantrum, demanded that MemMem leave. Luckily, she was soon able to find another family who needed a live-in housekeeper/nanny. She lived with that family for the rest of her life.

A few years after the war, my sister Sally was born, and I joined the family six years after her. In my early years, I was very close to my father, even a bit spoiled by him. This may have been because he was basically in grandfather mode during his mid-fifties. By this time, he was already slipping into alcoholism—fueled in part by PTSD from the war. He could be quite frightening to me when he drank, as he often did.

At five years old, I was an energetic child. But I was almost always willing to please my wonderful, loving mother. She was patient but also firm when she needed to be. One day, I overheard my mother and grandmother talking. MemMem was saying that she was planning to visit my oldest sister, Elise, who had recently given birth to her third son. MemMem wanted to meet the new baby. I was excited to hear this because my sister's two oldest sons were just slightly younger than me, and I loved playing with them.

I ran up to my mother and MemMem, asking if I could go, too. My enthusiasm was not deterred by their hesitation and doubtful expressions. My mother initially was against this because she knew that it would be challenging for her strict German-born mother to deal with my rambunctious energy. But for some reason, MemMem decided to take me along with her. I jumped for joy!

Over the next week before the trip, my mother repeatedly told me, "You better be good for MemMem." Each time my mother said this, I assured her that I would with all the heartfelt sincerity that a five-year-old can summon. I really wanted to please both her and MemMem.

I really had not been around MemMem very much before this. Prior to our recent move to Boise, Idaho, we had lived in California for the first five years of my life, and MemMem rarely visited us there. My mother frequently wrote letters to her mother. Wanting to emulate her, I would write too. My letters were pages of looping scribbles as I tried to copy my mother's cursive writing.

Whenever we visited MemMem, she required that I take an afternoon nap—usually, this happened when she became tired of me interrupting their conversations. During these "nap" times, I would lie on her bed staring at the clock and wishing the hands would move until they reached the time that I had been told I could get up. To this day, I've never been good at taking naps!

When the day for the trip arrived, MemMem and I boarded a Greyhound bus. As I started to climb the steps onto the bus, my mother reminded me again, "You better be good!"

I sat next to the window during the three-hour ride, feeling happy and excited. It wasn't long before I found it hard to sit still. A few times, MemMem asked me to "Stop touching me!"

After an hour or two, she exasperatingly grabbed my hands and tried to interlace my fingers. I didn't know what she wanted my hands to do until she finally succeeded in folding my hands in what I recognized as the "prayer" pose. I remember thinking, "Why didn't she just show me what she wanted?" I looked at my hands and thought, "How can my hands be bad when I am trying so hard to be good?" I was perplexed by this thought.

I was very excited to see Elise and my nephews when they greeted us at the bus station. Riding in the back seat of her light green station wagon with my nephews, I felt free from the cramped bus ride. This was before children's car seats, and we could crawl over the back seat into the spacious rear area.

Once at their home, my nephews and I were happily playing with cars and trucks on the living room floor. MemMem and Elise were sitting on the couch talking while MemMem held the new baby. I overheard a sudden change of tone when Elise angrily said, "I don't know why she doesn't leave him."

MemMem responded, "You know why. It's because of Christy (me) and Sally."

I knew they were talking about my mother, and I remember thinking, "I thought they loved my mother. Why would they talk about her in a mean voice?" But my next thoughts were even more upsetting. It had never occurred to me that my mother could leave. What if she did? MemMem said that she won't leave because of Sally and me, but I'm not there. What if she takes Sally and leaves? I thought that would be easier than taking both of us. It terrified me to think of being left alone with my father when he drinks.

I looked toward the two of them on the couch and thought, "I never want to be a woman. I never want to be like them." When I turned back toward my nephews, I felt like they were in another world completely and that I couldn't possibly rejoin them now.

I didn't know what to do with myself. I could hear my sister's husband, Glenn, making noise in the garage. He had just returned from a hunting trip. I really liked Glenn and thought maybe he would give me a much-needed hug. I walked toward the door to the garage. As I opened it, I immediately saw two female deer hanging from the rafters by their back hooves. My first startled thought was, "What if one of them is Bambi's mother, and her fawn is alone in the forest right now?" Being alone without a mother was so terrifying! I slowly walked toward Glenn, who sat with his back toward me while he talked with his neighbor. As I approached, I saw his arms covered in blood up to his elbows from the entrails of another deer on the table before him. I had never seen anything like this. I immediately froze.

The neighbor saw my terrified expression and sternly said, "You shouldn't be here." I turned away and walked into the house, not knowing where to be. I avoided everyone and went into the mud room at the back of the house. I leaned against the door jam, slowly sank to the floor, and cried without stopping.

I don't remember when someone found me, just that I couldn't stop crying. Later in the evening, I remember being held by MemMem in a rocking chair while she tried to console me. She didn't understand why I wouldn't stop crying and thought I was homesick for my mother, which was only partly true. At one point, Elise tried to reach for me to relieve MemMem. I pushed her away. She asked, "Why? Are you mad at me?"

Through my tears, I responded, "You said mommy might leave!" I'm not sure if she knew what I was talking about. I only understood that they all thought I was a homesick crybaby, just wanting my mother. I knew they thought I was "bad." Later, Elise put me down to sleep with my nephew at opposite ends of his bed. I tried not to wake him while crying until my pillow was soaked with snot and tears.

The next day, I could only wonder how I could be so "bad" when I had started out trying to be good. I decided that I could never help but to be a bad person, no matter how I tried to be otherwise. When Elise served deer liver for dinner that night, I couldn't eat it. I was told that I couldn't leave the table until I ate it, so I decided to sit there as long as they made me. I remember MemMem saying, "I know she likes liver." Maybe I had liked it before, but I have never been able to eat it since that day.

A few months later, my family moved to South Lake Tahoe, California. I was excited to begin school. I had missed kindergarten because, at that time in Idaho, kindergarten was only free for children born there. If there had been a fee, my parents couldn't have afforded it. Throughout first grade, I spent time almost every day standing in the corner for being "bad." It sort of became my safe place. I often didn't even know exactly what I had done to be sent there by our strict teacher, Mrs. Bell.

I was, however, very determined to learn how to read. I loved the new books and workbooks I was provided because I never had many children's books at home. I struggled hard to learn the sounds letters made and how to combine the sounds to make words. By Christmas, when MemMem came to visit, I had learned to master the letter sounds and most of the words in our readers. As a thoughtful gift, MemMem had thought that I would enjoy a small children's book in German. She sat next to me on the couch and began to read. I had never heard German or any language except English, so I didn't know what she was saying. I looked closely at the words in the book. I knew the letter sounds and what she was saying didn't match at all. I told her, "You're saying it wrong!"

She replied, "This is German." I had no idea what that meant and tried to sound out the words in the book myself. Frustratingly, she said, "You read it then." She walked away, and that was the last time she ever interacted with me.

It isn't always possible for us to have an opportunity to understand and change our early agreements with life. Often, such agreements become the way we interact with the world, even as adults–unless we find a good therapist! However, I was given a chance to transform my agreement that I was a "bad" person while I was still young.

When I entered second grade, I was lucky to have a wonderful teacher, Mrs. Greenough. One afternoon, she even made a home visit after I'd been in her class for a few weeks. Perhaps she wanted to talk with my mother to understand my difficult behavior.

Since I had vowed never to be a woman, in second grade, I decided to be a boy. This became more important after my protective big brother joined the Navy. I had decided that it was much safer to become more like him if he wasn't there. Unlike other schools in California at the time, our school in Tahoe allowed girls to wear pants to school since the winters were long and cold. I wore pants every day and began to sign my papers with the name "Davy," after my TV hero, Davy Crockett. Once, Mrs. Greenough told the boy passing out papers that Davy was me, even though my classmates knew me as Christine.

Another day, I did something wrong as the class was dismissed for recess. I don't remember what I did, but I remember that Mrs. Greenough called me over to her desk and asked after the class had gone, "Did you really want to do that? Is that what you actually wanted?"

I looked at her sheepishly and said, "No, not really." But suddenly, someone I respected had told me that I actually had a choice! I had never thought of myself as having a choice. I usually acted the way I did because I thought I was bad–as if it defined who I was. It was a revelation to realize that I didn't have to be bad if I didn't want to! I could now even choose to be good if I wanted to, and I decided to practice being good instead. Having a teacher who cared to give me a choice made all the difference in my world from that moment on.

Even though my grandmother never understood me (and I didn't really understand her), I see now that she played a more significant role in my life at a sensitive time than she probably ever realized. Of course, she never knew about the agreements I made with life that day or how they impacted my life over the next few years.

As I look back now with greater perspective, I realize that I actually made one other important agreement with life that day. In the moment when I felt most alone, I realized that I must ultimately rely on myself when others are unable to help me. I think that's why the rest of the visit with my sister's family went better. This self-reliance is a truly precious gift that has always resonated powerfully in my life. The challenges we meet in life are often the experiences that offer great rewards.

Today, I do feel a little sad that I didn't have more opportunities to share loving experiences with the only grandparent I ever knew. We never had a chance to know each other after that because MemMem always lived far away in Idaho–and then she died on the same day as my father when I was just 13. Since they disliked one another so much, I have often wondered what they might have said to each other if they had met that day on the other side!

About Christine Judal

Christine Judal has always been inspired by service. This inspiration has guided her through a variety of life experiences. During her decade as a teacher, she instilled a love for learning in her students, fostering critical thinking, self-esteem, and creativity. Transitioning into federal civilian service, Christine developed technical expertise as an Air Force Quality Assurance Specialist, ensuring aircraft components met rigorous standards. Her passion for safety led her to become an Environmental Health and Safety Specialist for the University of California, where she championed workplace safety and environmental protection until her retirement. When she was offered the unique opportunity to apprentice under don Miguel Ruiz, author of The Four Agreements, she was grateful to deepen her spiritual and personal growth. From don Miguel, she learned the value of changing our early agreements with life when they no longer serve our truth. As an author, Christine hopes to pass on this legacy, serving with a commitment to shine a light for others to find their own way home.

"Our ancestors live in our wounds. By healing them, we honor their struggles and transform our future."

– Unknown

www.ingramcontent.com/pod-product-compliance
Lightning Source LLC
Chambersburg PA
CBHW051537120626
46551CB00012B/1259